Your

MICHIGAN

WILLS, TRUSTS, & ESTATES EXPLAINED SIMPLY:

Important Information You Need to Know for Michigan Residents

By Linda C. Ashar, attorney at law

YOUR MICHIGAN WILLS, TRUSTS, & ESTATES EXPLAINED SIMPLY: IMPORTANT INFORMATION YOU NEED TO KNOW FOR MICHIGAN RESIDENTS

1405 SW 6th Avenue • Ocala, Florida 34471 • Phone 800-814-1132 • Fax 352-622-1875
Website: www.atlantic-pub.com • E-mail: sales@atlantic-pub.com
SAN Number: 268-1250

Library of Congress Cataloging-in-Publication Data

Ashar, Linda C., 1947-
Your Michigan wills, trusts, & estates explained simply : important information you need to know for Michigan residents / by Linda C. Ashar.
p. cm.
Includes bibliographical references and index.
ISBN-13: 978-1-60138-417-1 (alk. paper)
ISBN-10: 1-60138-417-3 (alk. paper)
1. Estate planning--Michigan. 2. Wills--Michigan. 3. Trusts and trustees--Michigan. I. Title. II. Title: Your Michigan wills, trusts, and estates explained simply.
KFM4340.A98 2010
346.77405'2--dc22

2010014485

PROJECT MANAGER: Melissa Peterson • INTERIOR DESIGN: Samantha Martin
FRONT & BACK COVER DESIGN: Jackie Miller • millerjackiej@gmail.com

Printed on Recycled Paper

Printed in the United States

We recently lost our beloved pet "Bear," who was not only our best and dearest friend but also the "Vice President of Sunshine" here at Atlantic Publishing. He did not receive a salary but worked tirelessly 24 hours a day to please his parents. Bear was a rescue dog that turned around and showered myself, my wife, Sherri, his grandparents Jean, Bob, and Nancy, and every person and animal he met (maybe not rabbits) with friendship and love. He made a lot of people smile every day.

We wanted you to know that a portion of the profits of this book will be donated to The Humane Society of the United States. ***–Douglas & Sherri Brown***

The human-animal bond is as old as human history. We cherish our animal companions for their unconditional affection and acceptance. We feel a thrill when we glimpse wild creatures in their natural habitat or in our own backyard.

Unfortunately, the human-animal bond has at times been weakened. Humans have exploited some animal species to the point of extinction.

The Humane Society of the United States makes a difference in the lives of animals here at home and worldwide. The HSUS is dedicated to creating a world where our relationship with animals is guided by compassion. We seek a truly humane society in which animals are respected for their intrinsic value, and where the human-animal bond is strong.

Want to help animals? We have plenty of suggestions. Adopt a pet from a local shelter, join The Humane Society and be a part of our work to help companion animals and wildlife. You will be funding our educational, legislative, investigative and outreach projects in the U.S. and across the globe.

Or perhaps you'd like to make a memorial donation in honor of a pet, friend or relative? You can through our Kindred Spirits program. And if you'd like to contribute in a more structured way, our Planned Giving Office has suggestions about estate planning, annuities, and even gifts of stock that avoid capital gains taxes.

Maybe you have land that you would like to preserve as a lasting habitat for wildlife. Our Wildlife Land Trust can help you. Perhaps the land you want to share is a backyard—that's enough. Our Urban Wildlife Sanctuary Program will show you how to create a habitat for your wild neighbors.

So you see, it's easy to help animals. And The HSUS is here to help.

DEDICATION

To my family.

TABLE OF CONTENTS

INTRODUCTION

Estate Planning: What Is It?

Many estate-planning books ask you to start by taking inventory of everything you will leave behind. When you are trying to plan for the time after your death, it does make a certain amount of sense. The problem is that you could end up with an extremely long list, including every single compact disc you own right now, not to mention the entire contents of your junk drawer — but to what end? You might have a sense of what matters to you most right now, but what about five months or 50 years from now?

Asking difficult questions and knowing what your priorities are will be the two most important parts of your estate planning. Whether you need a trust, additional life insurance, or a living will depends on what you want, not what a lawyer or an accountant tells you to do. But making those choices can be difficult, so these first three chapters are designed to walk you through the process of figuring out what you want.

Once you have a sense of what is most important, then you have a reason to dig into the details about wills, beneficiaries, taxes, and all that other minutiae to make sure the people and organizations you care about — not the courts or state and federal governments — benefit from your lifetime of hard work.

In this book, we provide a philosophy and common sense approach to estate planning to give you a place to start. The first part of the book gives a generalized overview of broadly applicable principles. As you will be reminded from time to time, the laws of your state control several aspects of estate planning and provisions for your property at death. *In Chapter 11, we focus on the specific requirements for Michigan residents.*

Throughout this book, you will see checklists, worksheets, helpful tip boxes, and case studies by professionals or people in your similar situation to help you with the process of planning your estate. *The worksheets referred to throughout the book can be found in Appendix A of this book.* There are also checklists and other interactive tools throughout the book that you should take advantage of.

None of the information provided in this book is intended to be legal advice. Each person's situation is unique and dependent on specific facts and circumstances. For the best legal advice, you must seek legal counsel from an attorney who is specially trained in the field of estate planning and trusts.

CHAPTER 1

Getting Started

"Men in my family live well into their 70s, so I have plenty of time to do this."

"I created a will when my children were born. They are the only valuable 'possessions' I have, and they are already taken care of."

"This is only my third year in a full-time job. I have student loans to pay off and make no money. I do not have an estate to plan."

"We have been married for 12 years. If one of us dies before we get around to doing our estate planning, the spouse inherits everything — everyone knows that."

"Estate planning is for old people."

This list of reasons for not doing any kind of estate planning is as varied and creative as the reasons concocted by children who did not do their homework. But unlike a teacher, who can excuse a missing paper, the state — the governmental body ultimately responsible for resolving all legal matters related to anything left behind by a person who has died — does not accept excuses from the next of kin: spouse, child, parents, or otherwise.

There are state and federal laws that tell a judge how to distribute the ownership of real estate, credit card debts, mortgages, cash, Grandma's antique end table, and the boxes of personal papers stashed in the attic. To make matters more confusing, each state has a different idea about how that ought to be handled, and Congress keeps changing the rules at the federal level.

According to estate planning professionals, all of those perfectly reasonable explanations for not doing estate planning are just excuses for avoiding two of the most taboo subjects in many cultures — money and death. With death comes the emotions of fear, denial, and anger. With money, there can be issues of self-worth, concern about the perceptions of others, and worries about the ability to support those who need help. These feelings combine to create an emotional quagmire.

Pile on top of all that the unfamiliar terminology, complicated tax laws, and a host of people who will take a chunk of your money planning for what happens after your death, and it is enough to make anyone want to say, "The dog ate my estate plan."

Estate Planning Simplified

Like all complicated tasks, the best way to begin is with individual pieces of information.

Estate planning is, in the simplest terms possible, creating a set of instructions about what should be done with your things — money, possessions, investments, collectibles, or anything you own — before and after you die. It is more than just a will that distributes your best china and savings accounts. It is more than a "to do" list someone can follow to pay off credit card bills, what you think is a good asking price for your house, and, after the house is sold, instructions for making sure Fluffy goes to a good home.

Anyone who has possessions, no matter how many or how few, needs to do estate planning. After you are gone, the mortgage payment still has to be made, and your favorite charity is still going to need a new roof, but you will not be there to write the checks. The bank and the charity will be sorry for the loss your family has experienced, but you need to determine how you are going to follow through on the commitments you made to those institutions.

This thing called estate planning is just a continuation of what you do now — sharing yourself, your money, and your life experiences with the people and organizations that are important to you. Estate planning allows you to make sure the money and property you accumulated during your life can continue to serve your purposes after you can no longer direct matters yourself.

You can do things with your estate before you die, but some things cannot be done until your death. There are technical things to consider, such as what taxes must be paid and how, in addition to distributing all your stuff. Before you can get to any of those details, you need to have an understanding of where you are in your life right now and the fact that it will end at some point.

Everyone Dies: A Simple Statement, Complicated Implications

Death is seen by some as an excellent adventure, the next step in living. For most people, thinking about death is not a fun thing. This is why dying and all the trappings related to it are not a topic that comes up between, "Pass the green beans," and "What's for dessert?" Given a choice between a conversation about death and doing dishes, people will fall over each other racing for the kitchen.

Like all things unfamiliar, the less we talk about death, the less familiar it is, and the more uncomfortable we feel when it does come up. Avoiding death and what happens to those who are left behind only makes those matters more frightening. Like learning mathematical equations or the periodic table of elements in chemistry, practice and repetition make the unknown familiar.

Numerous books focus on death and the process of dying. As these books have become more prevalent, some basic knowledge has crept into everyday language and consciousness. Dr. Elisabeth Kubler-Ross, who wrote *On Death and Dying*, popularized the acceptance of grief over loss as a perfectly reasonable thing. She used grief — the sadness and upset feeling over losing someone or something that is cherished — to create a list of the emotional stages people go through when trying to understand and accept a loss.

The Five Stages of Grief

1. **Denial and isolation.** Disbelief that the loss has taken place and possible withdrawal from familiar routines and people.
2. **Anger.** Feeling furious at the person who inflicted the hurt or at the world for letting it happen; upset with self for allowing the loss to occur, even if nothing could have stopped it.
3. **Bargaining.** Attempting to negotiate with a higher power, saying, "If I do this, will you change the outcome or bring about a miraculous solution?"
4. **Depression.** Feeling numb, lost, and unhappy. Anger and sadness may still be present.
5. **Acceptance.** All of the unsettled feelings calm down, maybe even fade, and the reality of the loss is finally acknowledged.

When just considering the loss of a loved one, these feelings can arise. That is also true of our own death. The advantage of facing these emotions is that you can use the opportunity to face the self-doubt, fears, and anxiety. You can also tally up the accomplishments, successes, and positive impacts you have had. By looking at all those things, you can develop a more realistic view that will allow you to value yourself and your efforts. By giving contentment a chance to grow and become stronger, you can gradually dissolve those fears and worries. You can also begin to see that, even if you cannot take it all with you when you go, the fruit of your labor can still be used to do the things you have already tried to make happen.

Money Talk

Most adults do not want to "burden" children with financial issues, but without age-appropriate participation in conversations about family finances, children will never be guided in their learning about the role and impact of money. This exclusionary approach turns money into an off-limits topic. It can also make money appear to be the cause of problems, a bad thing, or even a big secret.

By taking time to consider your past experiences with money, you can begin to understand the source of negative feelings or worries. You can also clarify in your mind the importance money has in your life right now. Decisions about the future are going to be difficult at best if you do not know what you want to accomplish — and disastrous if you make choices that are at odds with your true hopes and dreams.

One strong influence that can lead to misguided financial decisions is the "keeping up with the Joneses" mentality. Even if you do not think about painting your house to make it look as good as your neighbor's house, which was just repainted, you most likely notice who has just repainted their house, who has a new car, and who is going on vacation to the Bahamas. The amount of disposable income someone has can create a link between net worth and self-worth.

I Do *What* with All This?

The point of giving serious thought to death and money is to sort through the obstacles that keep you from doing your estate planning.

To keep all of this from getting too overwhelming, or if you are the sort who needs to do things such as collecting bank records to make you feel you are accomplishing something, consider using a practical, logical method for collecting and organizing these potentially emotional and volatile memories, experiences, and thoughts.

Lists

Create a list for each topic and organize the content into groups based on a common thread. Consider all possible angles for every topic, including past, present, and future. Be honest; nobody has to see these but you. Here is an example:

Money

Memories — childhood/family

- Mom and dad arguing about the mortgage at the end of every month
- Getting a piggy bank from grandma and money every birthday to "save for college"
- Handing the bank teller my savings book and a bag of pennies, and she smiled at me when she gave me a sucker

Memories — adolescence

- Lemonade stand: math class story problem turned Saturday afternoon project with friends figuring out how to pay for ingredients and cups, how much to charge, and splitting the "profits." (I made my first dollar.)
- Being the only one in the class who did not go on the trip to Washington, D.C., because dad was just laid off

Adult experiences

- My first car dying on the freeway and having no money to tow it
- Getting that first student loan payment book after graduation
- Photocopying my first paycheck

Dreams

- Owning my own home
- Paying for in-home care for mom and dad (so they do not have to live with me)
- Having three kids and sending them all to college
- Spending a year abroad before I die
- Not having to worry about paying bills every month (Is that even possible?)

Career versus Job

Memories — childhood/family

- Work ethic lectures from grandpa while cleaning out the garage
- Grandma: "Put off work until tomorrow if you can play today."

Memories — adolescence

- Summer car wash for school fundraisers being hard work
- Career counselor at school being insistent about engineering as career due to testing scores

Adult experiences

- Trying to make hobby of skateboarding into a business
- Intense dislike of all things entrepreneurial
- Feeling terrorized by bills

Dreams

- Have a job to make money to support the rest of my life
- Not owning so much stuff I need a storage locker to hold it
- Beach bumming at 50

Other topics to focus on can be death, family, career, play time/recreation, fears/worries, and anything else that evokes strong emotions as you consider other issues.

Journal

Choose a book or create a self-styled notebook (with lined or unlined pages) in which to record your estate-planning experience. Create sections for various stages in the process, leaving room for facts and figures, your feelings, and your thoughts. Allow space for doodling and pages of questions. Keep pages open for free association. For example, write "money" at the top of a blank page for space to just write down what comes to mind on that subject.

Stuff box

Recycle a sturdy shoebox or go out and buy a special storage box for the estate-planning occasion. Put in your lists, thoughts scribbled on the back of a napkin while drinking coffee, and your journal. This way, you can find all of those bits and pieces when you need them and create a physical place for the fragments that come to you, no matter what the form. If a movie ticket stub reminds you of the documentaries you want to make some day, toss it in. From these, you will be able to organize your questions and ideas into your planning journal and/or files.

File folders

If you are someone who functions better with more structure, create a folder each time you address a specific topic, including getting ready to do your estate planning. Photo prompts can be an amazing help in organizing thoughts and focusing upon goals. Choose a family photo or a picture from a magazine that illustrates what matters most to you, and tape or staple one into each folder. When you get frustrated or annoyed, look at those pictures to remind yourself of why the work is necessary.

Use index cards to jot down thoughts or digitally record your musings while you commute to and from work and on errands — the method does not matter, it is doing the work that counts. Once you identify the things that prevent you from planning for your retirement and death, you will be able to look more clearly at the present to help guide the future.

Here and Now

Beyond the tangle of complicated emotions and hang-ups related to death and money, you need to figure out what is most important to you so that you can set some goals for what you want to happen after you die. How to go about doing that effectively depends on the individual or people involved.

How one spouse views money can be dramatically different from the other spouse's perspective. The people and things each values may differ. What is valuable can be difficult to define because of the way culture places high importance on materialistic things. The following values analysis exercise is one way to begin identifying what matters most to you.

There are some things we feel we should say to be a good person, like, "Family matters most." There are also things we need to survive, such as food, water, and medical care. Both of those things can be important, but that does not make either of them a value we hold. To distinguish these points, consider the following definitions:

- Need: A requirement, necessity
- Want: To desire deeply, to wish for
- Value: To hold in high regard, to appreciate and rate highly

Once you can distinguish between your needs, wants, and values, consider the role that values play in your daily life. Those things that you value tend to serve as the test or measuring stick for making decisions. When planning a summer vacation, do you feel it is more important to get away from daily stresses and relax in quiet with your immediate family, or is going on vacation without your parents and siblings never an option? Do you make sure you never miss extended-family events such as weddings and graduations? You might value your extended family as highly as you do your immediate family, or your immediate family might be foremost in all decision making.

Stepping out of your everyday life to thoughtfully consider what makes up your everyday life is a way to gain perspective on what matters to you. Here is a values list to consider:

You

- Are you postponing something now — maybe learning to paint — because you feel something else is more important, such as tutoring for your children?
- Are you a spiritual or religious person?
- Do you want your kids to have everything you did not?
- Is your decision making impulsive or thoughtful?
- Do you have time every day to do something you want to do?

Family

- How many children do you have or want to have?
- What if infertility becomes an issue — do you want to adopt?
- Are you close to your parents? Siblings?
- What role does extended family play in your life?
- Are there any relatives with whom you are particularly close?

Friends

- Are you close to people who are like family but not related by blood or marriage?
- Is "guys'/girls' night out/in" scheduled on a regular basis?
- Do you consult with one or more people about big changes you wish to make?
- Do you follow the advice of anyone in particular?
- Whom do you trust with your children when you are away?

Money

- What matters most to you — having enough money to pay the bills or having extra cash?
- Are you living paycheck to paycheck?
- How much money do you save from each paycheck?
- What retirement savings do you have, if any?

Community

- Is attending city council meetings a priority?
- Do you pick up trash when you are out walking the dog?
- When do you check a community calendar, when you are looking for a garage sale or trying to find something to do on a weeknight?
- Do you belong to a specific religious tradition to which you give your time and talents?
- When was the last time you chatted with a neighbor?

The practical decisions to be made about your estate, such as who will get what, can gradually become clear as you sort out what is a feeling, what is important, and who is in your life. Instead of being caught up in whether the size of your estate will confirm your father's prediction that you would always be a screw-up, you can see how important he is to your family and that you want to do whatever you can to help care for him — before and after you die.

Separating facts from feelings will make it possible to see the opportunities and benefits that planning has to offer.

• *Did You Know?* •

At some point in time, most people have taken some kind of personality assessment test. In high school, they were designed to direct clueless teenagers toward a specific career path. Magazines claim to be able to identify your ideal mate based on a ten-question survey that identifies your personality based on the Myers-Briggs® typology.

When assessments to be used in the workplace gained popularity in the 1980s, your human resources department might have rolled out a company-wide assessment program to help mangers better understand and communicate with employees on a daily basis or to help them work through disputes. Lumped into one of four groups associated with a flavor of ice cream — "Are you a vanilla too? Bo is a chocolate, and Pat is a strawberry. No wonder my department is so messed up!" — the results seemed more gimmicky than informative and helpful.

Over time, research and development have refined and specialized these assessments to the point where the results provide surprisingly accurate, functional information about individual values and interests. If you are struggling with shifting priorities or feeling confused about how to deal with changes in your life, this one tool can offer some insight and direction.

Put This to Use

If you have trouble completing the values exercise worksheet or putting into words what you feel is most important in your life, taking an assessment might help.

Choosing an assessment tool can be difficult when you do not know where to look. The most reputable companies work with certified professionals — social workers, psychologists, coaches — whom they train to select the best assessment tools to provide the kind of information you need. The specialist will then discuss the results with you, asking questions and offering suggestions about how to use the results.

TTI Success Insights® is an assessment company that offers an inventory called Personal Interests, Attitudes and Values™. This is not a free service, but the information provided can be very useful.

What This Work Can Do

Change is difficult for most people on a good day, but under the influence of grief, it can be impossible to accomplish the most mundane tasks such as cooking meals and taking out the garbage. At some point in the future, your family and close friends are going to be in that same position.

Maybe your family will prefer to wear red, yellow, and bright orange to the memorial service. They might even make a family trip out of scattering your ashes on the Atlantic Ocean. Regardless of how your family will choose to cope with your death, there are things you can do to allow them the freedom to cope in the best way for them.

You can do things like plan out and pay in advance for your funeral, polish off the mortgage, cover your mother's assisted living bills so she can spend her retirement money on cruises, add a new wing to the church or community college, or set up a foundation to endow your community council's social justice efforts.

Estate planning can also help you now: By getting clear about your priorities now, you can plan and save in ways that will allow you to realize goals you envision for during your lifetime.

- Integrate and organize all your goals — personal, professional, financial, and estate.
- Preserve your assets for use now and in the future.
- Provide for your family and charities.
- Ensure the efficient distribution of your estate.
- Save money — taxes, legal fees, and court costs, for example.

What Exactly is Involved?

Each estate plan is different. Just as there are no identical people, there are no one-size-fits-all estate plans. There are similar components, and numerous books have been written about every possible aspect of estate planning.

Also, depending on where you live, laws come into play to affect what you can do with your property and when you can do it. This book is geared toward Michigan residents and the laws that come into play for those residents.

The chapters that follow will walk you through the basic process and then offer more detailed information about the elements of an estate plan before explaining how to prepare to create your own. This, like any other book or template, ought to be a resource for gathering information and generating ideas. To adopt a canned plan that is sold as "cheap and easy" is to get what you pay for, not the outcomes you hope to achieve.

This book will help you do your homework and learn enough terminology to ask questions of estate-planning professionals. If you want to do the job right, find people you can trust with your hopes and dreams.

What this book is *not* is a substitute for legal advice. We are providing general information for guidance, to assist you in planning how you want to arrange your personal estate for yourself and posterity. Laws change, and how they are applied depends on specific individual circumstances. Do not rely upon any statement in this book as specific legal advice. Using skilled advisers will help you address your specific circumstances and guide you on the status of the applicable federal and state laws.

CASE STUDY: HIRING AN ESTATE-PLANNING COACH

Patricia Beaugard, executive coach and trainer
pat@patbeaugard.com
www.patbeaugard.com

CLASSIFIED CASE STUDIES™ directly from the experts

Patricia Beaugard has extensive experience in the field of personal and professional coaching, in addition to being a trained ITT assessment specialist. She shares some of her thoughts on how a coach can be an important part of your estate-planning team.

Facing death

Many people have a difficult time facing the idea of their own death, so they avoid things that will remind them of it, like estate planning. Shifting the focus onto the people who are left behind — their survivors — is a way to focus on helping them. Ask, "What can I do to help my loved ones get through this difficult time in their lives?"

It can be helpful to look at what is bothering you: What is holding you back? What are your fears? All of these things indicate some underlying concerns; they might be related to dying, to money, or maybe to your family members. How much you are going to delve into these things is based on individual preferences.

Making notes about things you feel and the thoughts that come up when you think about estate planning can be part of the process of identifying what you have, to whom it will be given, and how your possessions will be distributed. And it needs to be a process: Make some notes and set it aside for a few days or weeks. Go back to it after you have had time to think about these things before you ask yourself, "Is this what I really want? Am I clear on this?"

Money, stuff, and meaning

Money represents something of value, because of what it can be used for. Actually, it is a form of energy. Many people work hard for their money and are attached to it — they might struggle with the idea of "giving it away" to others because it represents their work and accomplishments. For those who can see money as energy, it can flow to others because they can always get more.

People make decisions based on their emotions and their feelings. Sometimes they are not even aware of the feelings they have, so it can be helpful for another person to help them sort out those feelings. After you share your thoughts and feelings about a specific issue — like not wanting to distribute your estate — another person can share his impressions of your concerns. In that way, talking can help you explore how you feel and observe the influence those feelings have on your decision, or lack thereof.

Some people get quite passionate. That is when making time and space to step away and thoughtfully consider feelings and decisions is helpful; you can better determine whether that passion is a serious priority or a passing thing brought on by the estate-planning process. Consider:

- Where did this passion come from?
- Has this passion been a lasting influence?
- How have you lived this passion in your life?

I have a friend in Seattle who has never had children, but she has always had dogs, and all of them are rescued animals. For her vacation, she went to spend time with an organization in Utah that rescues all kinds of animals. She spent a week volunteering there, and she supports them financially. This is truly a value of hers because she supports it in word and deed.

Motivators and values

By looking more deeply at what matters to you — your values — you will find what drives (or motivates) you to choose the profession you are in, where you live, or the kind of volunteer work you do for which organizations.

Another way to approach this is considering who and what is important in your life: extended family, non-blood "relatives," faith or spirituality, hobbies, the things you collect, or the traveling you do.

For people who have difficulty talking about those things or identifying them, written assessments can help you identify your values in a concrete way. Do you care about making a difference in society? Not everyone does, but some people are quite driven by that. Are you focused on making sure your family has financial resources available to them, or do you value independence and want to foster that in your family? Maybe you see leaving your estate to your family as "spoiling" them.

What matters to you now might change in a few years — consider what you could not do without several years ago, for example, and compare that to your life now. As a result, revisiting your motivators and values on a regular basis is important, and a coach can do more than remind you to take that second, third, and fourth look — she can ask you the questions you might forget to ask yourself so that your review is thorough.

Finding a coach

A life coach helps you look at and consider these complicated, difficult topics in a constructive manner. When choosing a coach, you want to decide what criteria are important to you. Do you want to work with a coach that others have recommended? Do you want your coach to be certified? Do you want someone who has graduated from a coach training program? What kind of background or experience is important in your eyes?

Big Sable Point Lighthouse, Michigan

CHAPTER 2

Estate Planning Basics

According to a recent survey conducted by Harris Interactive:

- 55 percent of adult Americans do not have a will.
- 68 percent of adult African Americans do not have a will.
- 74 percent of adult Hispanic Americans do not have a will.
- 59 percent of adults do not have a living will.
- 62 percent of adults do not have a power of attorney for health care purposes.
- 10 percent of adults who have not prepared any part of an estate plan say it is because they do not wish to think about dying or becoming incapacitated.
- 9 percent of adults say they do not have an estate plan because they do not know who to talk to about creating one.
- 24 percent of adults say they have not created an estate plan because they lack the sufficient assets to require one.

The one thing these numbers reveal is that most people do not plan for their deaths or what happens to their money and possessions once they are no longer around to call the shots. Estate planning is not a mysterious, incomprehensible set of legal documents.

Even though estate planning does encompass a broad array of complicated issues, such as federal tax law and "heretofore" legal language required by the courts, you do not need to become an expert in all these areas. The most important thing to recall is the simple foundation on which all of this rests: When you die, you cannot take everything with you.

Sure, you can be buried with your platinum credit card or favorite jewelry, and you might even be able to arrange to be buried *in* your car, but the balance due on all of the above must be paid. Your debts, or liabilities, do not disappear — that is one part of your estate.

Your house, retirement funds, savings account, and family heirlooms still exist, too. Your son cannot claim to own the family house simply by saying, "She gave me the keys before she died and said it is mine." If you do not transfer the title to his name and the necessary taxes are not paid, then legally, the house is still yours. Those things that have a positive value, or assets, are the other part of your estate.

Without doing the necessary legal paperwork, your belongings are still your belongings — debts and assets — and the state will dispose of all of it because you are no longer around to do it yourself.

Beyond the stuff are the unexpected and potentially more complicated issues leading up to your death. A heart attack or car accident could result in brain death. Who makes the decision about your medical care and use of extraordinary means to extend your life?

The best way to ensure that your wishes are carried out is to make them known. That means learning the facts about what you can and cannot do.

Debunking Myths

People will do, say, and believe just about anything to avoid doing things they do not want to do; estate planning is no exception. Maybe that is how so many myths about death and taxes came into being.

- ***Myth:*** The estate tax — the "death tax" — was repealed, so there are no taxes to avoid any more. The federal estate tax law was repealed for one year at the beginning of 2010, according to a law called the Economic Growth and Tax Relief Reconciliation Act passed in 2001. If you happen to die during 2010, then you will not have to pay federal estate taxes, but your estate will still be subject estate taxes, if any, imposed by Michigan. The federal estate tax comes back in 2011, according to the same law as it currently stands. *There will be more information about taxes in Chapter 4.*

- ***Myth:*** All I need is a will — it will take care of all of my assets. Debts do not go away; even if a will sets aside money to pay those debts, if enough money is not set aside, then the inheritance you want for your child might go to pay your creditors first. A will only addresses property that is in your name — meaning your name is the only one listed on the title as the owner. Property that is owned jointly — a house, retirement accounts, or life insurance policies — will pass to the surviving owner, go to a beneficiary, or end up in the hands of the state if the ownership is not legally clear. *Chapter 5 goes into detail about wills.*

- ***Myth:*** Trusts are for wealthy people. A trust can be created by anyone and can include any personal property that you have. A trust can eliminate or dramatically reduce the amount of estate taxes that will be paid by your survivors and/or your estate, if it is set up properly. Choosing the right kind of trust to suit your needs and careful adherence to legal language will make a trust a viable option for anyone. *Chapter 6 explains all of this.*

- ***Myth:*** Life insurance is not subject to estate tax, so I do not need to do any other planning. Life insurance proceeds frequently are not subject to income tax if they are paid to someone else, like a spouse, parents, or a charitable institution. But if you own a life insurance policy and you have not named a beneficiary, then the proceeds of that policy become part of the taxable estate and will be subject to state and federal estate tax. Any person who receives the insurance proceeds will likely receive those proceeds without incurring any income tax liability. *Chapter 7 elaborates on insurance.*

- ***Myth:*** If I do not name a beneficiary for my 401(k), my spouse still gets the money. Assets that do not have a named beneficiary in a will or some other legal document will end up in probate court. If you want your spouse or some other person to have access to the unused portion of any retirement savings accounts, then they must be named as a beneficiary. Naming a second, or backup, beneficiary will also keep the account out of probate if the primary beneficiary is already deceased or declines the gift. *The way to incorporate your retirement accounts into your estate plan in discussed in Chapter 8.*

- ***Myth:*** If I die without a will, my spouse gets everything. In some states, this is true; in others, it is not. The laws of the state in which you live will determine who gets what, and creditors tend to be paid first. If you own property in two or more states — maybe a condo in Florida, a house in Michigan, and a cottage in New York — the laws of each state will be applied to the distribution of your real estate there. *Probate court and its impact on your estate are explained in Chapter 11.*

The list of misinformation or partial truths continues, with no signs of stopping. As estate tax laws change to close loopholes or take advantage of new revenue opportunities, the things you think you already know about estate planning can become obsolete without your knowledge. Over time, most people buy and sell things, such as houses and stock portfolios, and those changes mean that thing called an "estate" is ever changing, too. Whether your estate is growing or diminishing, you need to know what you have and how you want it to be handled after your death.

Your Estate

Yes, you have one, and defining it will most likely be the most straightforward part of this entire process. Your estate is made up of everything you own, or your entire worth in a numerical sense. The formula for figuring out your net worth — a person's true financial value — is simple:

Assets – Liabilities = Net Worth

Asset: Anything a person owns or is owed; this can be money, real estate, investments, or any other tangible property

Liability: A debt or an obligation to pay money to another person or institution; also called a negative balance

Following are some examples of common assets and liabilities:

Assets

- Annuities
- Cars
- Cash
- Certificates of deposit
- Insurance
- Investments
- Personal property (jewelry or household items, for example)
- Real estate
- Rental income
- Retirement funds
- Savings/checking accounts
- Stock certificates
- Structured settlements (lottery winnings or lawsuit settlements, for example)

Liabilities

- Bills/debts:

- Alimony
- Automobile payments
- Child support
- Credit card balances
- Future debt (a child's college tuition or care of parents, for example)
- Student loans
- Insurance premiums
- Mortgages (first and second home equities)
- Personal loans
- Taxes

Because it is important to keep your list of assets up to date, you might consider using a digital camera to make a visual inventory of your assets so that you can create an archive of these items. When documenting a dollar value for each, such as the appraisal of a necklace, you can scan that appraisal and make it part of the electronic archive. You can also collect and scan any other documents, such as stock certificates or a house deed.

These documents will be essential when meeting with estate-planning advisers, so collecting them in a secure, fireproof safe as you build your inventory will save time later.

People

You never know how many friends you have until you win the lottery; the same can be true about your death. Some people never know how many creditors, lost family, and/or illegitimate children they supposedly had until their will is made part of the public record. After you are legally declared dead, your will must be entered with the probate court, and it then becomes public record. Anyone who wants to make a claim against your estate can do so, and that is when the real work begins for those who helped you with your planning.

To make sure your wishes are understood and carried out, you need to make sure the people who are connected with your estate planning do as you choose, not what is most convenient for them.

Paid professional planners — those who carry out your wishes, such as executors, secondary executors, or legal guardians — and others — such as the probate court or judge, creditors, and beneficiaries — will have a say in what happens after you are gone. Some people you have no control over — you do not get to choose your probate judge — but others you do, so choose people who will help you even when you are no longer around.

Estate planning professionals

Yes, there are people who voluntarily do estate-planning work. What might seem like torture to you is a challenging, rewarding career for someone who likes helping people sort out and plan for the complexities of making sure death does not mean the end of their influence in this life. The fees they charge can be an hourly rate, a per-document fee (for a simple will, approximately $300), or an ongoing estate-management fee. Be sure you understand what the charges are and how they are paid, and, if there is a contract, read the fine print.

Lawyer

Also called attorneys, lawyers can specialize in specific aspects of estate planning, such as wills, trusts, or probate court, or they might have a broader focus, such as estate planning or tax law. Depending on the size of your estate, you might need to consult with more than one lawyer to make sure all the legal issues related to your estate are properly prepared for. Some law firms have different team members who can do all your work in-house under the direction of your lawyer. Or, you might feel more comfortable having different firms work on different parts of your estate plan. No matter how you approach this, you need to be forthcoming about all your personal goals and estate-plan wishes with everyone involved so that the work on the various areas support, not undermine, each other.

Certified Public Accountant (CPA)

Accountants can specialize in various aspects of financial estate matters, such as trusts, annuities, and estate tax law, but they also serve as estate-planning specialists who can help you consider all financial decisions. An accountant must be current on tax law and other legal requirements related to accounting for money. Like a law firm, an accounting firm can have several people on staff who specialize in different areas. But the same caution applies: Be comfortable with your CPA, because he or she has to be trusted with all the same personal information if he or she is going to work well with the others on your team.

Financial planner

There are all kinds of financial planners out there with initials after their names — Certified Financial Planner® (CFP®), Certified Financial Advisor (CFA) — and some without initials. But all of them analyze a person's overall financial situation and then develop a comprehensive plan, in conjunction with the individual, which will attempt to meet his or her financial goals and objectives. Planners who are certified have followed a specific course of education or training classes, and some go on to develop expertise in specific areas such as estate or retirement planning. Financial planners can help you prepare your estate for after you are gone, but they can also help you build up the kind of estate you want to leave behind. Be wary of anyone who is self-taught or who works on 100 percent commission — the advice you get might not necessarily be based on the most current information or in your best interest.

Insurance agent

Gone are the days when an insurance sales rep showed up at your door and offered to spend hours chatting with you about your insurance needs — home, auto, and life being the basics. Today, many reps go through human resource departments to communicate long-term and short-term disability coverage, which might or might not be partially paid for by the employer. Medical and dental insurance — not to mention pet insurance, long-term care insurance, and other less common insurance plans — are now sold over the phone or the Internet. An actual insurance agent can help you with your estate planning by assessing the kind and amount of insurance you need and can afford. An actual agent over a call-center staffer is the best way to go to make sure you get what you need, but if you cannot find one, your other estate-planning professionals might be able to help.

Coaches

Financial, professional, and personal coaches can help you identify and manage monetary, career, and personal goals. At a time when mixed messages about being loyal to your employer and diversifying your stock portfolio make you wonder what you ought to do about the stock options your company offers, a coach can help you sort out the implications of selling or keeping those options and the potential impact on your career and estate plan. Their goal is to see you succeed, not make sure a corporation thrives or your beneficiaries get a chunk of change. A coach can be the ultimate disinterested third party. Again, training and comfort level are critical to finding someone who will be a good fit. There are certification courses for various forms of coaching, but there are no national standards, and formal training is not required to present oneself as a coach.

Spiritual adviser

The altruistic efforts of many people are based on their chosen faith traditions or their own moral compasses. Making difficult decisions about personal matters is not necessarily something you are going to want to discuss with your accountant. Trying to decide whether your drug-addicted brother will be helped or hurt by a large inheritance might be part of your estate planning. Choosing charitable institutions to benefit from your life's work might also be necessary. Changes in your life, such as divorce or the unexpected death of a loved one, might necessitate changes in your will at a time when the family member you would normally discuss those things with is grieving. A minister, priest, monk, or some other cleric or individual trained in a specific faith tradition who offers guidance, support, and information related to your belief system can be helpful in these situations. Someone to talk to about personal matters related to financial decisions can offer a balanced view grounded in the highest ideals that you share with another.

Whether you need any or all of these people to participate in your estate planning is up to you. While some do not charge anything, others might have flat rates or hourly charges. The money you invest, much like the time you invest, is valuable, so be sure you weigh the short-term costs against the long-term gains.

If it looks as though you are going to need a number of people to help with your estate-planning details, consider choosing one person to serve as the primary contact through which all information will flow. If you choose a lawyer to serve as your point person, he or she would work with the other professionals on your team to collect and ask for clarification about their part of your estate management. Then he or she would meet with you and, at one time, go through all of the information. A time-saving efficiency for you, this will cost a little extra because you need to pay your lawyer to do this coordination work, but in the long run, you will have a reliable, well-informed person who can serve in your stead when you are gone.

☑ Choosing an Estate Planner

Estate planner qualities and characteristics:

Qualifications for estate-planning professionals will vary based on their professional focus and expertise. Individual training is important, but there are some fundamental skills that all of them ought to have. Scrutinize prospective estate-planning team members before and after you meet with them — they will be privy to your most personal and private information.

Before: Do some homework before you meet with a planner.

- ☐ **Is your estate planner ethical?** Check with the Better Business Bureau and any related professional organizations, such as the American Bar Association for lawyers, to find out whether any complaints have been filed or reprimand proceedings have taken place.

- ☐ **How well does your planner interact with clients?** Get references for current clients to inquire about the positives and negatives of working with this person. Some questions to ask his or her current clients might be:
  - Is this person prepared for meetings, and does she follow-through on tasks that need to be done afterward?
  - How well does this person collaborate with other estate-planning professionals?
  - Do you spend much time in the waiting area before an appointment?
  - Have you ever had mistakes occur with your invoices?
  - Have your meetings ever been canceled on short notice?

- ☐ **What professional associations is your planner a part of?** If this person is the member of an organization, call and inquire about his or her involvement and whether the organization can make any referrals.
- ☐ **What services does your planner offer?** Find out the range of services this person offers or whether he or she works in collaboration with others inside or outside his or her company.
- ☐ **Is your planner considerate?** Being willing to listen to your concerns and needs is essential; review his or her website or any promotional materials for signs of this trait.

After: When you meet with an estate-planning professional for the first time, pay attention to the level of comfort or discomfort you feel, and evaluate that meeting soon after. These are a few questions to consider:

- ☐ Did he or she ask you relevant questions?
- ☐ Which did he or she do more, talk or listen?
- ☐ Did he or she tell you what you should do or present you with options to consider?
- ☐ Did he or she disclose any commissions or other considerations he or she receives from the institutions offering the products he or she represents? For example, he or she presents three different kinds of life insurance; for one of those, he or she will receive a commission if you sign on the dotted line.
- ☐ Did he or she explain things in a way that you could understand?

- ☐ Was he or she willing to go back over things until you were clear about confusing points?
- ☐ Were you given fees and hourly rates in writing?
- ☐ Are you expected to sign a contract?
- ☐ Were you given a timeline or some other expectation about how long this process might take?
- ☐ Did you feel you were being helped, or was it seen as nothing more than a revenue stream?

CASE STUDY: WHAT IT TAKES TO BE A FINANCIAL ADVISER

U.S. Department of Labor
Bureau of Labor Statistics
www.dol.gov

Estate planning is a specialty within the field of financial planning, and the U.S. Department of Labor, via the Bureau of Labor Statistics, predicts this is going to be a growth industry for many years to come.

Beyond that, the bureau also provides job descriptions and other information about various industries, including financial advisers and planners. This material provides a description of the kind of work a planner might do in a day and the characteristics of a person who is successful in this kind of position. You might not be looking to make a career change, but this can serve as excellent background material when you begin looking for an estate planner to help you develop your plan.

Financial analysts and personal financial advisers

Significant points:

- Good interpersonal skills and an aptitude for working with numbers are among the most important qualifications for financial analysts and personal financial advisers.
- Keen competition is anticipated for these highly paid positions, despite rapid job growth; those who have earned a professional designation or an M.B.A. are expected to have the best opportunities.

- Almost one-third of personal financial advisers are self-employed.

Nature of the work:

Financial analysts and personal financial advisers provide analysis and guidance to businesses and individuals in making investment decisions. Both types of specialists gather financial information, analyze it, and make recommendations. However, their job duties differ because of the type of investment information they provide and their relationships with investors.

Personal financial advisers assess the financial needs of individuals. Advisers use their knowledge of investments, tax laws, and insurance to recommend financial options to individuals. They help them identify and plan to meet short- and long-term goals. Planners help clients with retirement and estate planning, funding the college education of children, and general investment choices. Many also provide tax advice or sell life insurance. Although most planners offer advice on a wide range of topics, some specialize in areas such as retirement and estate planning or risk management.

Personal financial advisers tend to work with many clients, and they often must find their own customers. Many personal financial advisers spend a great deal of their time making sales calls and marketing their services. Many advisers also meet potential clients by giving seminars or lectures or through business and social contacts. Finding clients and building a customer base is one of the most important aspects of becoming successful as a financial adviser.

Financial advisers begin work with a client by setting up a consultation. This is often an in-person meeting where the adviser obtains as much information as possible about the client's finances and goals. The adviser then develops a comprehensive financial plan that identifies problem areas, makes recommendations for improvement, and selects appropriate investments compatible with the client's goals, attitude toward risk, and expectation or need for a return on the investment. Sometimes this plan is written, but more often, it is in the form of verbal advice. Advisers sometimes meet with accountants or legal professionals for help.

Financial advisers tend to meet with established clients at least once a year to update them on potential investments and adjust their financial plan to any life changes — such as marriage, disability, or retirement. Financial advisers also answer clients' questions regarding changes in benefit plans or the consequences of a change in their jobs or careers. Financial planners must educate their clients about risks and various possible scenarios so that the clients do not harbor unrealistic expectations.

Most personal financial advisers buy and sell financial products, such as securities and life insurance. Fees and commissions from the purchase and sale of securities and life insurance plans are one of the major sources of income for most personal financial advisers.

Education and training:

A bachelor's or graduate degree is required for financial analysts and is strongly preferred for personal financial advisers.

Employers usually do not require a specific field of study for personal financial advisers, but a bachelor's degree in accounting, finance, economics, business, mathematics, or law provides good preparation for the occupation. Courses in investments, taxes, estate planning, and risk management are also helpful. Programs in financial planning are becoming more widely available in colleges and universities.

Licensure:

Almost all personal financial advisers need the Series 7 and Series 63 or 66 licenses. These licenses give their holders the right to act as a registered representative of a securities firm and to give financial advice. Because the Series 7 license requires sponsorship, self-employed personal financial advisers must maintain a relationship with a large securities firm. This relationship allows them to act as representatives of that firm in the buying and selling of securities.

If personal financial advisers choose to sell insurance, they need additional licenses issued by state licensing boards.

Other qualifications:

Strong math, analytical, and problem-solving skills are essential qualifications for financial analysts. Good communication skills also are necessary, because these workers must present complex financial concepts and strategies. Self-confidence, maturity, and the ability to work independently are important as well.

Financial analysts must be detail-oriented, motivated to seek out obscure information, and familiar with the workings of the economy, tax laws, and money markets. Financial analysts should also be comfortable with computers, as they are frequently used in doing work. Although much of the software they use is proprietary, they must be comfortable working with spreadsheets and statistical packages.

Personal financial advisers need many of the same skills, but they must emphasize customer service. They need strong sales ability, including the ability to make customers feel comfortable. It is important for them to be able to present financial concepts to clients in easy-to-understand language. Personal financial advisers must also be able to interact casually with people from many different backgrounds. Some advisers have experience in a related occupation, such as accounting, auditing, insurance sales, or brokerage.

Who Will Carry Out Your Wishes in Your Place?

After you are gone, someone has to take responsibility for what was once yours. This means people and property. Who will serve as the legal guardian of minor children is a huge decision and a tremendous responsibility for the person/people who agree/s to be responsible for the health and well-being of your children. A guardian of a minor, any adult legally appointed to be responsible for the needs of your children until they reach legal age, is not the same as a guardian for an adult. The guardian of an adult is any adult who can be legally appointed to manage the affairs of an incompetent or infirm adult of any age. A mentally challenged 32-year-old brother can need a guardian as much as a parent in the early stages of Alzheimer's disease.

Equally important is the executor of your estate. An executor, also called a personal representative, is the individual who handles the property you are leaving behind. If you die without a will, the court appoints an administrator — frequently a spouse or child. This person will make sure your assets and liabilities are disposed of in a legal, efficient, and thoughtful manner. The money necessary to support your children, a disabled sibling, or your aging parents will be in the hands of your executor.

Legal guardians

Whether for a child or an adult, appointing the guardianship of another person is legal action: The court appoints a guardian based on the wishes of the person making the request. A child's godparents do not automatically become guardians upon your death; you have to put guardianship in writing in a will. If you are the legal guardian of your elderly mother, you need to make provisions for her care in your will in the event that you might die before she does.

The guardian for a minor will be responsible for things like food, clothing, and shelter. However, he or she also will be responsible for managing assets in the child's name and providing for things such as education and health care. The same can be true for the guardian of an adult, who might also be responsible for paying bills and making sure the home is cleaned on a regular basis.

Choosing any guardian is difficult because of the responsibilities involved. The most obvious concern is selecting someone who will care for your family the way you would, but more important is whether the person will follow through on the commitment. A person in her 20s in the midst of building a career might say she is willing to set aside her career to care for her sister's young children, but after three years, will she still be willing to stay at home with the kids, even though money is not an issue?

Consider some of the following:

- Age: Young and old are as much about experience as birth date. Do you want the person taking care of your children to be your same age?

- Lifestyle: Your sister is non-religious, but you want your children to attend a Catholic church. Will she take them to church every Sunday?

- Child-rearing/caring-for-adult skills: Patience is essential, as is the savvy to know where to find and seek help as needed. Is the person you are considering good with kids?

- Marital status: Your divorced brother is fabulous with your boys, but would two parents be better for your children? Would your sister and her husband be better?

- Compatibility: If your kids hate your sister's husband, this is not going to be a good long-term fit. How do your kids act around the person you are considering?

- Money skills: Your aunt is a penny pincher, but your uncle is a spendthrift. Will the money set aside for your brother's group-home bills last under their watch?

You also need to consider your expectations for your children and how much of those you want to impose on the people who will become their new parents. Once you come up with the priorities you have for your children, make a list of several people and then ask each of them whether they would be willing to serve as guardians under the conditions that you lay out. It is a bad idea to name someone as guardian without his or her knowledge. If he or she refuses, the court will then decide what is in the best interest of the minors or others in need of care. The people the court chooses might not be to your liking.

A secondary or "backup" guardian will address the gap left by people who might be unable to serve in that capacity.

• *Did You Know?* •

A property guardian or property manager is a legal adult who takes responsibility for the oversight of property inherited by a minor/child. Children under the age of 18 can inherit property, but they are only allowed to legally own that property with adult supervision; an adult must have the responsibility of managing it. Just because a 17-year-old can inherit a car does not mean he or she is "in charge."

The responsibility of becoming the legal guardians of a minor child or children might be enough for the people you select to provide for their upbringing. If the burden of managing their property on top of that is too much, another person can be appointed for that role.

Put This to Use

Harry and Sally set up an education trust for their three minor children — Huey, Dewy, and Louis — in addition to putting the house and all other assets in their names. They are enrolled in private schools and will continue to live in their home; Aunt Blanche is moving in with them. Blanche has a good heart but is bad with money, so bad that she forgets to make her own house payment. Putting her in charge of making sure the tuition is paid from the proper accounts and the property taxes are paid on time is a disaster waiting to happen. So, Harry and Sally named their long-time banker and trust officer, Bill Smith, as the property manager. He also knows Blanche, so she can easily call him to ask for help if any additional school fees need to be paid. This frees her to focus on the boys instead of on the finances.

An added bonus is that Bill Smith, as a trust officer for a bank, is not likely to get away with embezzling money from the trusts. Bill cannot be paid a fee, which means more money for the trust.

☑ Choosing a Guardian

You, your children, a sibling, or a parent might one day need another person to make decisions that you — or they — would normally make. Asking someone else to take on your responsibilities in addition to their own is a significant request that carries legal, ethical, and moral implications. This is a brief list of things to consider when making a list of people you might want to ask to serve in this capacity:

- ☐ **Eligibility:** Different states have different rules about this. In Michigan, appointments are pursuant to court proceedings. If you move, be sure to check whether your named guardians are still allowed to serve.
- ☐ **Common ideals:** People who have similar views about child rearing, values, and religious beliefs are more likely to raise your children or care for your adult family members in the way that you would.
- ☐ **Compassionate:** There could be a need to address the emotional and practical issues and needs that come up as a result of your death.
- ☐ **Flexible:** Different people react differently to dramatic changes in life, so it might be necessary for the guardian to take time off work or move to a new home to be available to address the needs of his or her charge.
- ☐ **Emotional stability:** Grief is a reasonable response to death, but a person who is prone to depression or has mental health issues might not be able to care for others during such a critical time.
- ☐ **Marital status:** Some people prefer that children have a two-parent family; others are more focused on the personality of the guardian, and maybe being single means being more flexible. Consider what is most important to you, and be true to that criterion.
- ☐ **Location:** If the guardian is unable to move into your home or be close to his or her adult charge, those entrusted to them might have to move, and that could create additional stresses for already stressed people.

Things to keep in mind...

- Some family members might not be happy with your choice of guardian or might believe they are the best choice. Be prepared to address fears, concerns, and frustrations, even anger, from those who disagree with your choices.
- *Always* discuss the expectations and responsibilities with the potential guardian before naming that person in a will or other legal document.
- If it makes you both feel more comfortable, spell out your expectations of each guardian in writing so that you are both clear about your wishes.
- *Always* choose secondary and tertiary guardians in the event that unexpected situations (your first choice dies before you do) or life circumstances (serious illness or a job transfer to another country) make it impossible for that person to agree to be a guardian.
- Be aware that the court might decide that your choices for a guardian might not be suitable — maybe your brother was recently arrested on drunk-driving charges — and choose another guardian based on what the judge thinks is in the best interest of the child or person in need of a guardian. This is where naming secondary and tertiary guardians can be helpful in guiding the court.

Executor

Just as you need to select your guardians carefully, you need to consider who will manage the affairs of your estate, as opposed to running off to the Cayman Islands with everything in your trust funds. *See Chapter 5 for more information on the responsibilities of an executor.* The following list offers a quick summary of his or her duties:

- Guiding your will through the probate process to make sure it is accepted as valid. This also means defending the will against any challenges.
- Collecting your assets

- Overseeing the transition of gifts made to beneficiaries. This might include a title transfer for a house or making sure a life-insurance policy check is made out in the correct name.
- Reviewing, evaluating, and paying any claims against your estate. These commonly include taxes and outstanding bills that are owed.
- Raising the money to pay claims. This can mean selling assets, such as a house or car.
- Preparing and filing an accounting of all financial transactions for the court

The person who takes on this task must know what is involved. For this reason, choosing a secondary executor is a good idea; if you do not appoint one, the court will appoint one for your estate.

☑ Choosing an Executor or Trustee

The choice of an executor or a trustee is a highly personal decision, so there is no cookie-cutter definition or approach. Some things to consider are:

- ☐ **Integrity:** Can you trust this person, no matter what?
- ☐ **Your relationship:** Does this person know you well enough personally and professionally to know how you think and might want things handled?
- ☐ **Personable:** How will this person deal with a grieving family when decisions must be made?
- ☐ **Thoughtful:** Will this person consider questions and demands made on your estate by creditors, beneficiaries, the court, or anyone contesting your will and wishes?
- ☐ **Common sense:** When given multiple choices, does this person tend to be practical?
- ☐ **Realistic:** If this person does not know what to do, will he or she seek the advice of experts?

- ☐ **Potential conflict of interest:** Could decisions made by this person benefit others, including your trustee/executor, and harm your family?
- ☐ **Asset management skills:** What kind of experience does this person have with real estate and financial markets, for example?
- ☐ **Real estate management skills:** Is this person informed about what it takes to maintain and manage property in your estate, be it a house or undeveloped piece of land?
- ☐ **Knowledge of beneficiaries:** Can this person accurately assess the needs of your beneficiaries without your day-to-day guidance?
- ☐ **Criminal background:** Has this person ever been convicted of a crime related to the responsibilities you are asking of him or her?

Additional considerations/notes: ______________________________

____

____

People of Influence

After you are gone, the people who will have the most influence over what happens to your estate, in the legal pecking order, are the probate court, creditors, and your beneficiaries.

Probate court judge

Specifics about how probate court accepts, records, and addresses issues with wills are addressed in Chapter 11, but here is some information about how the court operates.

Probate court is part of a state's court system, as in Michigan. A listing of Michigan's probate courts is available at http://wcpc.us/links/michigan-probatecourts_address.htm. Regardless of the laws governing the organizational structure of the court, a probate judge will review the legal documents related to an estate. If a person dies without a will, the judge will appoint an administrator, who serves in the same capacity as an executor.

He or she also will ask for and review things, such as the will (if there is one), the inventory of assets, and petitions from creditors and heirs. Heir is the legal title of a person who inherits property from an estate that does not have a will, or is intestate; beneficiaries are those who receive an inheritance by being named in a legal document such as a will or trust.

The judge will supervise the process of settling your estate and will only adjudicate, or hand down decisions, as they are needed, such as when a creditor makes a claim and is denied payment by the administrator. The same can be done when a person comes forward and claims to be an heir to your estate.

The judge might choose someone you think is unsuitable for the job of administrator, and he or she might agree to pay the claim of an old business partner that you do not feel is owed. You can prevent these items from happening by creating an estate plan and avoiding probate when possible.

Probate judges also establish guardianship and handle other special circumstances, such as bigamy, live-in lovers who want part of an estate, or long-lost children who contest decisions regarding heirs.

Creditors

Your debts get paid first. So, how much you owe other people at the time of your death will determine how much of your estate goes to your loved ones and charities. Some creditors might not make a claim against your estate. Maybe you borrowed $5,000 from Aunt Henrietta, and she does not care about being paid back, so when your executor writes a check, she tears it up and hands it back.

Outstanding credit card balances, a personal line of credit from a bank, and a car loan are just a few examples of the bills you might be paying when you are alive, and these must be settled after your death. In addition to letting creditors know about your passing, your executor will request the amount of payments necessary to settle your accounts. Some companies, upon reading a death notice, might try to make a claim of payments due. It is up to the executor or administrator — or the probate judge, if this becomes necessary — to determine whether a claim is legitimate and must be paid.

Beneficiaries

Even if you die intestate, which means to die without leaving a will, there are a number of will substitutes that will make it possible for your estate to avoid probate completely: joint ownership of property, wherein the surviving partner automatically takes full control; revocable and irrevocable trusts; life insurance, pensions, and annuities with named beneficiaries; and stocks, bonds, and bank accounts paid to a designated person upon the death of the owner.

If a beneficiary is not named, or the primary beneficiary declines the bequest or is dead and a secondary beneficiary is not named, then the probate court judge will decide who receives the unclaimed property.

Beneficiaries and court-named heirs can challenge decisions made about an inheritance — whether you or the court makes that decision. People who believe they ought to have received an inheritance or who only received a fraction of what they were told they would get — or think they deserve — can challenge the will or court ruling. These challenges can hold up the resolution of your estate for months or years, so making sure your legal documents are in order can help reduce this problem.

These basic elements of an estate plan describe what is involved and who is integral to the process. Next are the components of an estate plan — the documents, accounts, and policies that make it all legal and taxable.

CASE STUDY: DETAILS AND LEGALESE DO MATTER

Scott M. Slovin, Esq.
Schwartz Manes Ruby & Slovin
sslovin@smrslaw.com
www.smrslaw.com

CLASSIFIED CASE STUDIES™ directly from the experts

What are some estate plan essentials?

The biggest concern in an estate plan is coordinating all of the estate plan documents, such as the will, with the trust and beneficiary designations, as well as ownership of assets, including payable-on-death or transfer-on-death-type assets. Essential information includes the following:

- The name of the testator (the person preparing the will) or the grantor or settlor (the name of the person creating the trust) of the trust
- Beneficiaries' names and relationships to the testator or the grantor as well as alternate (contingent) beneficiaries, should a beneficiary predecease the testator or grantor
- The fiduciaries (the executor or trustee) and the guardians for the minor children
- How estate taxes and other expenses of the estate will be paid and from which assets the cash will be drawn

The benefits of working with an attorney are to avoid mistakes in drafting — such as unclear bequests or failure to specify from what assets taxes will be paid — and to reduce federal and state estate taxes that a non-estate-planning lawyer and/or a non-attorney will fail to take into consideration.

Why is it important to use legal terms in estate-planning documents? So many of them are confusing.

There is a long history of interpretation under state law and federal tax law, and attorneys like to use language that they know has been interpreted by the courts to achieve the results they are seeking for clients.

Attorneys are trying to simplify their language and create wills and trusts that are easier to read and for clients to follow.

How does a person go about choosing a professional in your field?

The best way to choose an estate-planning attorney is to seek the recommendation of financial planners, accountants, and insurance agents who work with estate-planning attorneys. Make sure you choose someone who does more than a couple of wills per year. You need to find someone who spends at least half of the time in estate planning so that he understands all of the nuances of state probate and estate law, as well as tax law. Especially important would be attorneys who have extra training in the field of estate planning and tax planning. Recommendations of friends and neighbors would also be important.

A Dutch windmill in a field of blooming tulips in Holland, Michigan

CHAPTER 3

Components of an Effective Estate Plan

Car keys, directions, map, water bottle, and snacks: Planning for a road trip is easy because the basics of what you need are easy to identify and collect. The car does not go anywhere without the keys, and directions are essential for reaching the final destination. How you plan to achieve the goals of your estate planning can be equally simple, once you know the things that are necessary.

Like taking a road trip to a new place, there are plenty of guidebooks and maps prepared by those who have gone on this trip before — ranging from specialized and highly trained professionals to those who have learned from personal experience. Those people can help you do the things that will make your trip unique for you, and there is no need to use up much time and energy figuring it all out on your own. The components of an effective estate plan are all the same; what individualizes each plan is which pieces match your goals and how those components work together.

There is much legal language involved, but there are everyday words you can use for the same thing, just like a road that has a state route number (SR 56), a formal name (Lillian Paulsson Memorial Highway), and what the locals call it (Lil's Lane). Sometimes, knowing the description of something is good enough to gain the necessary understanding — i.e., "property is stuff you own" — so that you can find your way when the map gets confusing.

Legally Speaking

A court only recognizes legally binding documents as the way to give your estate to others. Some of these are so widely known and commonly used that descriptions and definitions hardly seem necessary. Most people know what a will is and what it is for. But the difference between what makes a document truly legal, as opposed to what you think is legal, can get you into trouble: If you do not have the right wording, enough witnesses, or the right witnesses, all of your efforts can be ignored.

The following are reoccurring terms you will find throughout this book:

- **Property**: The things you own, which can be anything you want to give to other people; also referred to as principal

- **Real property**: This is any kind of real estate.

  - ***Types:*** Vacant land that you buy with the intention of building on, or it might just be an investment that you plan to sell later without developing; your primary residence; a second home, such as a vacation condo; a portion of a home, such as a time-share; investment property, such as a two-family house you own yourself that generates rental income; or property in which you share ownership with a partner or business.

- **Personal property**: Your possessions. This category is further divided into tangible personal property — things you can touch — and intangible personal property, or financial assets.

  - ***Tangible:*** Jewelry, artwork, furniture, china, collectibles such as figurines or antique books, electronic equipment, cars, and boats

  - ***Intangible:*** Checking accounts, savings accounts, money market funds, mutual funds, stocks, bonds, or retirement accounts such as a pension, an individual retirement account (IRA), a Roth IRA, or a Keogh plan

- **Property interest**: This refers to the connection you have to a specific item, piece of land, or other belongings.

  - ***Legal interest:*** This is property you can legally transfer or manage, but is not yours to use or keep for yourself. Someone who is responsible for the maintenance and oversight of the use of a piece of property, but does not legally own it, is called a trustee.

    - *Example:* Steve manages the house and grounds of his great-grandmother Julie's family home because she lives in a nursing home. He calls a plumber and contracts to have work done so that the backed-up drains are fixed. Steve might even place an ad in the paper to rent the house, screen applicants, and then serve as the primary contract for the renter, collecting rent and addressing problems. But the property is in Julie's name, and Steve cannot sell the house or any of the land because it belongs to Julie.

  - ***Beneficial interest:*** You receive a benefit from the property.

    - *Example:* Veronica always wanted to go to art school, but she thought the tuition was too expensive, even with student loans. After she graduated from high school, her grandfather told her he had set up a trust fund for her, and the proceeds from that trust will pay her tuition and fees for art school.

- **Ownership**: What the individual or individuals who hold the legal title to a piece of property have. The ability to retain, sell, or give away this property depends on the number of people who hold that title (in some cases, it also depends on their relationship) and any legal agreements/contracts connected to the property.

- ***Sole ownership:*** A single person holds the title to the property.
  - *Example:* Mandy owns her car because she paid cash for it, and the title of the car is in her name.
- ***Joint ownership:*** When any two people hold an equal share of the title to a piece of property. The most common form is spousal — i.e., when a legally married couple has both names on a title to a piece of property.
  - *Example:* Joe and Mary are listed on the mortgage and the deed to the home they live in together.

- **Community property**: A state law that views a wife and husband as equal partners and assumes a 50/50 split of ownership. (Michigan is not a community property state.)
  - *Example:* When Clyde and Bonnie divorced, everything they owned that was not a specific gift from a family member or something either owned before or after the marriage was lumped together and divided into two equal parts.
- **Separate property**: Things that are owned by one spouse that are not part of the couple's community property.
  - *Example:* Fred owned an antique Model A before he and Carrie married, and the title is in his name.
- **Joint tenancy**: A group of people hold equal and undivided title to a piece of property. Joint tenancy is recognized in Michigan.

- *Example:* Brian, Joseph, and Greg own a cottage together in Michigan. All of their names are on the deed to the property, and they schedule their vacation time so that everyone has an opportunity to use the cottage.

Exemption: A specific amount of money that will not be affected by estate taxes. Federal taxes and states with an estate tax often set an amount, such as $1 million, that is tax-free. Taxes would then be due on $1,000,001 and beyond. There is no Michigan estate or inheritance tax, currently, for deaths occurring after December 31, 2004 and before January 1, 2011.

- ***Donor:*** The person who gives a gift or bequest

- ***Beneficiary:*** The individual(s) or group(s) that will receive the property in a will or trust. This can be a single person (a nephew), a group of people (all grandchildren), one group (Stray Cat Rescue Inc.), several groups (all community councils in your city), or a combination of any of these.

- ***Distribution:*** The disbursement or payment of property from an account to a beneficiary. It could be in the form of a check of some other monetary payment, or it could be the transfer of a title into the name of the beneficiary.

You will see many of these terms throughout this book, and some definitions will be expanded upon in sections that provide more detailed information.

Defining Your Estate

Understanding what property is and how ownership is determined now makes it possible for you to define your estate. Making a list of what constitutes your estate and what makes up the estate of a spouse or life partner will make it easier to understand some of the choices you have for creating your own plan.

This list, combined with the fundamental values you defined in Chapter 2, will help you consider how a specific estate-planning component might be a good tool for you. There are many choices to make, and it will not be possible to make final decisions quickly, but having some information about your estate in mind while you learn can make the process go more smoothly.

Pass the Parchment

Many important books and legal documents were printed on parchment. Only the wealthy could read, write, or afford to buy parchment for their private use or for special occasions, such as drafting the Declaration of Independence. Even though most of the documents that make up your retirement plan will not have the same historical impact as that document had, it is important to make sure the documentation you do is complete and accurate. If you forget a clause or use the wrong word, the directions you leave will not be worth the paper they are printed on.

What the document is, what it can do, and the laws affecting each will help you choose the elements of your estate plan that will transform your thoughts and wishes into action.

Will

What it is:

A legal document in which you identify the people or institutions that should receive money and property from your estate after your death. It also serves to appoint guardianship of children or adults who are your legal responsibility and designate an executor to manage your estate after you die.

What it does:

- It spells out your instructions and wishes for what you want done with the property you leave behind.

- Your affairs go from being private to public when you use a will because it becomes a part of public record — if you want privacy, keep your will basic and legal. *For more information on this, see Chapter 5.*

The laws that matter:

- State laws govern the execution of the instructions in a will.
- A will can be challenged and directions contained within it overturned by a judge.

Potential problems:

- Thinking a will is unnecessary or is all you need. Each extreme limits your estate plan's effectiveness.

- Using a will form from the grocery store or the Internet. Unless you know the laws of Michigan and how the language of that document matches up, you could have a false sense of security about what will happen after your death. *Will requirements for Michigan wills are discussed in Chapter 11.*

Will substitute

What it is:

An agreement, contract, or other legal arrangement that accomplishes the same goals of a will — to protect and transfer property rights — but without the use of a will document. Some options are:

- Holding property in a living trust or joint tenancy
- Payable on death account — the ownership of a monetary account, like a savings account, which is set up to automatically transfer the ownership of the beneficiary upon the death of the donor.
- Financial arrangements that have a named beneficiary — life insurance, IRAs, or pension plans.

What it does:

- These arrangements can save time because the ownership automatically transfers to the beneficiary upon the death of the donor, so it skips the probate process.
- Privacy is preserved, again, because the substitute does not go through probate and is not subject to open records laws.
- They can also save money because probate court fees are not needed, and some estate taxes can be avoided.
- An unconventional situation — such as multiple ex-spouses and blended families with children from previous marriages — might be better addressed with a will substitute.

The laws that matter:

- Tax laws of Michigan and the federal government; there is a significant amount of misinformation about what is tax-exempt and what is not.

Potential problems:

- Missing details — each form of will substitute has its own quirks and legal requirements; not having enough signatures, witnesses, or clauses could nullify the entire document. Using the wrong language can also submarine your efforts.
- Find a qualified professional to help you close all the holes in your documents.

Trust

What it is:

A legal arrangement that involves the transfer of property from the original owner to a person or company. The trust holds and maintains the property for the benefit of a specific individual, group of people, or institution(s).

What it does:

The legal arrangement will hold any property in a tax-free account until distributions are made to people or institutions other than the donor, depending on the kind of trust and the beneficiary, or until the entire trust is turned over to a beneficiary.

The laws that matter:

- Taxes, again. Some trusts are tax-exempt; some taxes must be paid by the beneficiary when distributions are made or the ownership of the trust changes from your name to the beneficiary. Be sure to know what the tax implications are; not all trusts are created equal.
- Exemptions also apply here — trusts for education, a spouse, and for other reasons can eliminate taxes in the distribution or transfer of a trust.

Potential problems:

- Choosing a trust that will not achieve the results you want. Many sales reps will make a commission off the trust you establish, so they might be looking at how to maximize their profit.
- Thinking a trust is all you need

Insurance

What it is:

A method of protecting valuables in the form of a policy in which premiums are paid over time to guarantee a specific payment for a specific purpose by the company accepting the premiums. Those valuables can be property — home, car, jewelry — a person's life, or the ability to work and care for yourself — life, disability, health care, long-term care.

What it does:

- These various policies protect an estate from the devastation an unexpected accident or terrible illness can bring to your finances. They can preserve your assets and allow you to spend/distribute them as you choose.

- For a small investment, insurance can dramatically increase the value of your estate.

- Some insurance policies only pay a percentage amount — long-term disability might only replace 50 percent of your pre-disability income — so what you receive depends on another factor, like your income.

The laws that matter:

- Taxes, again. Know what insurance income is taxable — disability insurance payments, death benefits, and other kinds of insurance might be subject to local, state, and federal income taxes and/or estate taxes, depending on the age of the beneficiary.

Potential problems:

- Buying more insurance than you can afford; once you stop paying premiums, the policy will no longer pay benefits.

- Believing that buying insurance is all the estate planning you need to do

Taxes

What they are:

Estate taxes are fees levied by federal and state governments against property that is left behind after a person dies. Gift taxes are fees levied by federal and state governments against property that is transferred to someone before the owner dies.

What they do:

Taxes affect the amount of money your beneficiaries do or do not receive, because all bills, including taxes, get paid out before your beneficiaries see a dime. Carefully investigate what taxes must be paid on the property you leave behind and who is responsible for paying.

The laws that matter:

- All kinds of loopholes were created and filled over the years, so federal and state tax codes in particular can be extremely confusing. It is impossible to provide a specific list.
- This is where a professional is essential to avoid fines, late fees, and other charges on top of the taxes already owed.

Potential problems:

- Thinking that you will not have to pay any taxes after you die. You might not be around to write the check, but that does not stop the government from sending a bill.
- A failure to leave instructions for your executor about money you set aside specifically for the purpose of paying your estate's taxes could result in the sale of assets or other mistakes in the management of your affairs.
- An executor failing to file your final income tax and the necessary estate tax forms can have serious consequences for your executor and the bequests you want others to receive.

Retirement funds/pension

What it is:

Money saved in different kinds of accounts with the intention of using those funds to pay for living expenses after a person is no longer employed full-time. There are employer-sponsored accounts — profit sharing plan, stock bonus plan, employee stock ownership plan (ESOP), and 401(k);

individual accounts — IRA, Roth IRA, annuity, variable annuity, or Keogh plan; and government benefits in the form of social security retirement benefits, Medicare, and disability.

What it does:

- Funds saved for retirement are supposed to make it possible for seniors to live comfortably without working, but planning and the right kind of saving are essential to achieving that goal.

- There are no guarantees: Just because you save does not mean the money will be there. As more companies renege on retirement plans and under-fund employer pension contributions, the retirement you think you will have might not be possible.

The laws that matter:

- There are serious financial penalties imposed on funds removed from retirement accounts before you reach retirement age.

- Social security benefits are taxed as income.

Potential problems:

- Believing that government benefits will be enough to live on when you retire.

- Pension plans that are not insured might not deliver the benefits promised.

In the end, your estate plan might look similar to that of your spouse, or it could be completely different. It all depends on the things you value most and how you handle financial matters. Here is a bumper-sticker summary of how your estate plan might look:

"Fly first class; your kids will, after you are gone."

Ferdie and Lilly, married 65 years with three grown, independent daughters

Will: Separate wills, written at the same time, leaving everything to the surviving spouse with specific bequests of heirlooms to family and sentimental tokens to friends, with everything else going to the church in which they were married after both are gone

Living will: Instructions to not use any extraordinary life-sustaining efforts should they experience a loss of brain function or a disease that impairs their ability to make sound decisions

Life insurance: One policy was already cashed out to pay for an Alaskan cruise. A second policy will be used to pay for funeral expenses for the first who dies, and the last policy will be used for the survivor.

Pension plan: Spending the dividends every month; whatever is left goes into the travel fund.

Living trust: Spending the dividends every month and using the rest for road trips

Charitable trust: All property is held in trust for the church and the animal rescue and shelter.

"Yours, Mine, and Mine."

Andrea, divorced with no children and living single for more than 40 years

Will: Does not have one; Andrea lives on a houseboat that she rents, and all her possessions fit into whatever car she leases, so there is nothing to bequest.

Living will: Does not have one

Life insurance: Three policies — one for mom, one for dad, and one for all death-related expenses

Disability insurance: Short-term, long-term, and extended-care insurance policies

Retirement accounts: Her 401(k), Roth IRA, and stock bonus plans will cover her monthly expenses, and whatever is left goes into a rainy-day account.

Trust: Her cabin and land she owns on Whidbey Island in Washington, where she plans to retire

"The one with the most toys wins!"

John Richard Greenman XIV, and Maya E. Primwater, not married but living together for 18 years, no children — his and hers estate planning

John Richard Greenman XIV

Will: Fifty percent of everything not in trust goes to Maya — just enough information in the will to make it legally binding and uncontestable.

Living will: Instructions on how to use or refrain from using any and all extraordinary life-sustaining efforts. Michigan recognizes this concept only for the designation of someone else to make decisions for a person who becomes incapacitated, as designated in the form of durable power of attorney for health care.

Life insurance: Multiple policies with multiple beneficiaries including parents, siblings, long-time family servants, and a few elderly female relatives

Retirement accounts: All set to roll over into trust funds to support the educational efforts of all subsequent generations of nieces and nephews, contingent upon achieving specific grade point averages, with financial rewards for exceeding those levels

Living trust: Spending the dividends every month on lavish parties, resort vacations, and redoing the summer house in the Hamptons

Charitable remainder trust: Several specific charities get the "leftovers," which will be approximately $11 million.

Social security: Benefits will go to support arts organizations.

<u>Maya E. Primwater</u>

Will: 50 percent of everything not in trust goes to "Johnny" — just enough information in the will to make it legally binding and uncontestable.

Living will: Instructions to use no extraordinary life-sustaining efforts

Life insurance: Multiple policies with multiple beneficiaries, including siblings, lifelong friends, and charities

Retirement accounts: All set to roll over into an endowment fund to provide ongoing support for more than two dozen charities and nonprofits for which Maya volunteers

Living trust: Spending the dividends every month on visits to overseas nonprofit organizations doing research for her endowment

Education trust funds: Several funds are set up to send her nieces and nephews, cousins, and the children of close friends to study abroad; other funds are set up for "self study" for those who want to find their way in a less academic environment.

Social security: Benefits will go to support local social justice groups.

Whatever money is left in her retirement accounts is to be placed in trust after her death to establish a writers' retreat that will be operated by the Write on the Sound Writer's Conference.

By looking over these hypothetical estate plans, you can begin to see how the things you value might impact the decisions you make.

• Did You Know? •

The person who will eventually administer your estate has some basic guidelines to follow due to state and federal laws regarding this task. Specific taxes must be paid by certain deadlines. An extension can be granted, but only if the paperwork is completed in a certain way, submitted to the correct office, and signed by a specific person or judge. You can help make this process flow a little more smoothly by keeping that in mind and planning for some potential problems.

☑ Watch Out for This!

Prepare a letter with details about how to administer your estate.

- ☐ Provide as much detailed information as possible about your estate. Annual updates to your documents will mean fewer undocumented items for the executor to track down.
- ☐ Bonding requirements for your executor can be waived if you include language in your will to that effect. If your executor is a bank, you might want to keep those in place, but for a family member, this might not be necessary.
- ☐ Death notices must be published at least once in a newspaper in the county of the deceased's residence and also sent to known creditors or claimants of the estate, who have four months to make their claims after notice is provided.

Your executor should be aware of the following things:

- ☐ Publish the death notices properly to avoid disputes.
- ☐ Be diligent in identifying and inventorying assets; an apparent lack of effort can result in legal trouble.
- ☐ Ask questions about anything that is unclear in legal documents and estate administration instructions and get clarification in writing. This can help avoid potential disputes or help address those that do arise.

Things neither of you control:

- ☐ Disputes raised by creditors or dissatisfaction about how a claim is settled
- ☐ Disagreements between and challenges brought by beneficiaries
- ☐ Claims made by a spouse against an estate that conflict with the terms of a will; some states, including Michigan, entitle a spouse to a specific percentage of an estate regardless of the decedent's wishes.

CASE STUDY: COMPONENTS OF AN EFFECTIVE ESTATE PLAN

Anne Marie Griffith
Tom Kotick
SS&G Financial Services, Inc.
Certified Public Accountants
and Advisers
tkotick@ssandg.com

What is essential to include in an estate plan?

Estate planning is the process of developing and implementing a master plan that facilitates the distribution of your property after your death and according to your goals and objectives.

The critical pieces involved in estate planning involve the following documents: a will; a trust in the case of minor children, a large estate, or second marriage with children from prior marriages; durable powers of attorney; a living will and a medical power of attorney or medical proxy;

and a letter of instructions is recommended. Other critical priorities of the estate-planning process involve the selection of an executor/executrix for your will/estate, a guardian for your minor children, and trustees or co-trustees in the case of any trusts created. Finally, a cash-flow analysis and some income tax planning should be part of the priority list for the estate-planning playbook.

Anyone with property or minor children should have a will. While most people think of the will as the driving factor determining where your property goes, beneficiary designations and the titling of assets often play a bigger role in this determination. For example, when someone owns property as joint tenants with rights of survivorship, this property will go to the joint owner, regardless of what a will says. Also, many assets are governed by beneficiary designations, such as retirement plans and life insurance. These types of assets will always pass by way of the beneficiary designation, not according to a person's will.

Life insurance is one of the biggest players in the estate-planning game. For some, it is the only way to ensure that family members will be able to support themselves after the death of the primary wage earner. For those with larger estates, life insurance can provide the funds needed to pay estate taxes (and other costs) without liquidating estate assets. For those with a business interest, life insurance can be used as a vehicle for business succession. Finally, for those with a generous spirit, life insurance can permit you to make charitable gifts.

What are the most common mistakes people make? What do people forget to include?

A very common mistake is not addressing the estate-planning process at all, which can result in what is called "dying intestate," or dying without a will. In that case, the distribution of the estate and the care of minor children are resolved by the state.

Another oversight is not funding the estate to properly care for your spouse or your minor or school-aged children in terms of ongoing financial needs for daily living and future educational costs.

Other common mistakes or oversights are in the need for annual income-tax filings for any trusts that have been created or gift-tax return filings in the case of gifts over the annual exclusion amount.

What are the benefits of working with someone in your field?

A CPA who is experienced in working with clients on their personal financial plans, which include estate planning, can help avoid the mistakes and oversights mentioned previously.

The CPA can effectuate the "quarterbacking" of the estate-planning process. This is done in several ways, including assisting the attorney in drafting the documents in accordance with the client's needs and desires, as well as recommending a good estate attorney if the client does not enter the process with an attorney; coordinating the work of the investment/broker to properly identify and re-title assets; and working with the life insurance agent to make sure ongoing living and educational expenses are covered with the right amount and type of life insurance coverage and policy.

The CPA is usually involved in the preparation of any annual trust or gift tax filing requirements that might spring from the planning process.

The CPA will gather the information necessary to make the filings by coordinating the assistance and necessary input from the other team members to make the proper filings each year.

How does a person go about choosing a professional in your field?

If a client is working with a CPA for his annual personal and/or business accounting and tax work, you can start by asking if she does estate planning as well as income taxes. Or you can ask your CPA for a referral to a CPA who is experienced in the financial-planning process involving estate planning.

It helps qualify the CPA if he/she has certain additional certifications, such as the PFS (Personal Financial Specialist) designation, or a CFP® (Certified Financial Planner®). Also helpful is a CPA who has studied for and retains a state life-insurance license.

Mackinaw City Bridge, Michigan

CHAPTER 4

Taxes

When Roman Emperor Caesar Augustus was running short on cash to pay for things like aqueducts and parties, he created the first estate levy. Ever since then, death and taxes have been linked. Unfortunately, our version of that original tax law has become complicated and confusing over time.

When one loophole is discovered, a new rule is created to cover it. But then that rule has a little wiggle room that needs to be closed up, so another rule is created — and the cycle continues. So, do not count on an easy answer to the question of how much tax money your estate will have to pay after you die. Your best bet is to track down people who specialize in tax law — a CPA and/or an attorney.

The gross estate, which is the value of all property owned by the deceased person on the date of death, is what gets taxed. The federal government gets a chunk based on the Estate Recovery Act, the estate tax, referred to as the "death tax" by those in Congress who want to completely do away with it. Some states have a state estate tax similar to that of the federal government, though other states levy a tax on the property received by the beneficiary — an inheritance tax. All these taxes have a host of exemptions or deductions that reduce or eliminate the taxes that need to be paid. As noted previously, there is no Michigan estate or inheritance tax, currently, for deaths occurring after December 31, 2004 and before January 1, 2011.

Strategically using the exemptions and deductions and creating tax-free accounts makes it possible to get around some of these taxes. That is one of the best benefits of estate planning. Before you can save taxes, you need to know what they are and how much you might owe. Without a crystal ball or clairvoyance, it is impossible to know what the precise worth of your estate will be at the time of your death, but planning for what you do know puts you in a position to help your loved ones avoid some painful tax bills.

Bear in mind that no matter how much you prepare, the tax laws can be changed with the stroke of a pen in Washington, D.C., or Lansing, and everything you thought you knew and planned for can be changed. Consider all the information in this section to be accompanied by an asterisk, which means: subject to change at any time, so do not consider this information to be the definitive legal authority.

Check with a tax professional who is current with federal and state tax law changes.

Federal First

Three federal taxes directly affect your estate: the gift tax, the generation-skipping transfer tax, and the estate tax.

Any gift you give to another person or institution — in cash or the transfer of property — in one fiscal year is subject to a gift tax. There is one exemption: the first $13,000 given to any single person or organization is exempt from the tax, but everything from $13,001 and beyond is subject to being taxed.

- *Example:* You decide to give niece Meghan $5,000 as a high school graduation present because she wants to tour Europe before going to college.

- *Do you owe?* No. Because this gift is under $13,000, you do not owe any taxes on this gift.
- *But...* You can only give Meghan another $8,000 this year and have it be tax-free. If you make the next gift $9,000, you will owe the gift tax on $1,000.

As the donor, the person who gives a gift, you are eligible for some tax deductions that might also make the tax bill go away. The donee, the person or institution receiving the gift, is what determines the deduction or exclusion you can apply:

Tax deductions — your spouse, many charities
Exclusions — medical expenses, political organizations, tuition

- *Example:* Your husband has an opportunity to buy a workshop full of woodworking tools from an elderly neighbor who is giving up the hobby. He has his own checking account, but it was his turn to add money to the kids' college fund this month and he does not have enough cash. So, you give him the money from your checking account.
- *Do you owe?* Nope. The marital tax deduction means you can give your spouse $150,000 in a year, and it is tax-free.
- *But...* If you try to do the same thing with the man you have lived with for 18 years and are not married to, you will have to pay the gift tax on $137,000. You still get to take advantage of the annual $13,000 exemption.

Like all things, these deductions and exclusions all have fine print. To have an unlimited, tax-free marital deduction, your spouse must be married and a U.S. citizen at the time the gift is made.

- *Example:* It is Friday night, and grandson Thomas calls, absolutely frantic. His tuition is due the following week, and he cannot reach Mom (she is out of state at a convention). Dad has not been around for years — and even if he were, he almost certainly would not have the $13,200 he owes. You write down the name of the school, address, and all of the particulars so that you can have your bank transfer the funds on Monday.

- *Do you owe?* No. For the education exclusion to be on the up-and-up, the gift must be paid directly to the educational institution, so you will not owe any taxes.
- *But...* The education exclusion is for tuition or training only. Thomas is on his own for books, unless you give him additional cash.

Charities must be qualified by the Internal Revenue Service (IRS). You cannot just give money to an animal shelter and deduct that from your taxes. You have to make sure the IRS has decided it is a charity, and the gifts you give to a charity need to fit into predetermined categories:

- **Outright charitable gift**: This is property that you give to a charity without getting anything in return. The gift can be cash or any other type of property.
- **Bargain sale**: The sale of a piece of property to a charity at a rate that is below the fair market value. The difference between the amount paid and the actual value is the amount of the gift.
- **Stock bailout**: The transfer of stock ownership from your name to that of the charity. The fair market value of the stock at the time of the transfer is the gift amount.

Many other conditions must be met to make your gift tax-free, regardless of who gets the gift. That is why you must consult with a tax expert to make sure your interpretation of your gift matches what the government allows. Unless you are a whiz at tax law, you are in all probability going to need some help navigating the ever-changing federal estate tax.

In 2001, a law called the Economic Growth and Tax Relief Reconciliation Act was passed that increased the exemption for the estate tax. In 2002 and 2003, taxes were owed on anything over $1 million. So, if your estate was worth $1.5 million, you only had to pay tax on $500,000. At a 45 percent tax rate — the highest federal tax rate for an estate — the exemptions create a limit to the money the feds can collect. The exemption increased to $3.5 million until 2009. The tax was repealed, but later reinstated with an exemption of $5 million for 2010 through 2012.

For a while, some people managed to dodge the estate tax dilemma. A person with a multi-million-dollar estate did not want to have less money to give to her beneficiaries, so she named her grandchildren or great-grandchildren as the beneficiaries. They are all minors, so they do not have to pay any taxes on their inheritance. But the federal government caught on to that and created a tax specifically designed to tax the money skipping over generations. Called the generation-skipping tax transfer (GSTT), it is the most complex tax law, according to the experts in the field.

There are entire books written about this topic, and they still do not encompass all the details. Suffice it to say, if your estate is worth more than $2 million, you will want to work with an estate-tax planner to make sure you look at the implications of trying to give all your worldly goods to the youngest of your family tree.

• *Did You Know?* •

Children under the age of 14 are required to pay income tax at the single person tax rate on income earned through employment. They must file a tax return like everyone else, but they get "special treatment" by the IRS if their parents are wealthy and try to give a large sum of money. "Kiddie Tax" is the term used to describe income tax applied to money that minors did not earn through employment, also called unearned income. In 1996, a special law was created to close a loophole that allowed parents to give their children a large gift as a way to pay a lower tax on the interest earned. The child tax rate was significantly lower than the adult rate.

The law has changed over the years, and in 2008 it changed again. The first $900 in income made on any investment in a child's name — age 19 and younger, extending to the age of 24 if the child is in school full-time — is not subject to income tax. The next $900 is subject to a 10 percent tax, up to $90. Anything above $1,800 is taxed at the tax rate of the child's parent(s).

☑ Watch Out for This!

- ☐ You can take advantage of your child's lower income-tax bracket by investing in U.S. Savings Bonds. The income is deferred and so are the taxes.
- ☐ Money paid to your child in the form of wages for working in your business is not subject to the "kiddie tax." Those payments are deductible by your business, but it is important to keep the necessary records for hours and work performed. Not having these could make it appear as though you are trying to cheat on your business taxes.
- ☐ A child earning her own income and paying taxes can still be declared as a dependent on a parent's tax return, allowing that parent to take a standard deduction. If you divorce and do not get custody of the children, you do not get "custody" of the standard deduction for your taxes.

Now for the State

The state wants to get some of that estate you are leaving behind, too. Some copy the federal law and have created a state estate tax, which means your estate has to pay taxes on the property you leave behind. Because these taxes are tied to the federal tax, you need to make sure you are looking at the most current, correct federal estate-tax tables to know what Michigan estate tax will be as the laws change.

Other states levy a tax on the property received by a beneficiary — an inheritance tax. The structure of these taxes will depend on the state law, but as a rule, the closer the relationship the beneficiary has to the deceased, the lower his tax will be. For example, a sister will have a larger exemption and will therefore have a lower tax rate than a distant cousin.

Some states also impose a state gift tax. To find out whether your state has such a tax, whether there is an annual exclusion, lifetime exemptions for close family members, or for any other legal technicalities, a good place to begin is the Michigan Department of Treasury.

Then there is the state income tax. You can be a full- or part-time resident, or simply live in the state for a few months out of the year and be subject to that state's income tax laws. Income earned in another state might be taxable in Michigan, which has an income tax.

Mistakes Happen… Frequently

The only federal regulation that might be more complex than tax law is immigration law. This complexity is why people make costly mistakes, miss savings opportunities, and wind up confused about what can and cannot be done legally. Most tax specialists are CPAs or lawyers, and it is their job to stay ahead of the latest changes to the ever-growing tax code.

Over time, some common mistakes related to taxes and estate planning have emerged. This list is a sample of those errors; they can help you identify holes in your own planning, help you prepare for a meeting with a tax adviser, and, at the very least, inspire you not to get careless about managing this element of your own estate plan.

Mistakes your executor can make include:

- Using the wrong IRS forms when filing taxes. This can involve consulting the wrong tables and filling out and submitting the wrong schedule — like using the 1040 EZ income tax form when, by law, you are required to use the 1040 long form.
- Missing information about your estate. If you do not provide or disclose all the information, your executor might not know oversight that occurs. The "But he didn't tell me" defense will not work.

- Not having the necessary record to justify or back up the filing. This can mean having no mileage record and missing receipts and account interest statements.
- Preparing a return without professional help. Professionals who are up to date on all the current tax laws can help an executor avoid a multitude of mistakes, such as using the wrong form or insufficient documentation.
- Miscalculations. This can involve transposing numbers or just coming up with the wrong number when adding or subtracting.
- Not signing the tax form.

Decision-making mistakes you can make while preparing an estate plan:

- When to bequeath a gift: before or after death
- How to use gifts that fall below the annual gift tax exclusion amount ($13,000 for 2010)
- The most advantageous way to structure a life insurance policy
- Selecting a trust with the maximum tax advantages for you and/or the beneficiary
- When it is best to leave property to a spouse?
- Whether to make a bequest that will negatively impact the tax position of the beneficiary

If you want to look up a specific topic or try your hand at sorting, the rules related to a specific estate-planning element — such as trusts — refer to **www.irs.gov**.

When, Not If, You Pay

The number-one benefit many professionals give for estate planning is dramatically reducing the amount of taxes that will be paid out of your estate. However, the only way to accomplish that is to know the tax laws of Michigan, any state in which you own property, and the tax implications of the way you choose to save and distribute your estate.

There are some helpful things to know about taxes when doing your estate planning:

The federal estate tax rate is subject to change by Congress; it is best to check where those rates stand every time you review or change your estate plan just to make sure you have enough money available to cover the bill, if you are not going to leave that job to your loved ones. You can put a provision in your will to pick up any taxes for your beneficiaries if you want to, but a lawyer is going to have to help you with the wording to make that possible.

It is the job of the executor of your estate to handle all these money matters. In addition to calculating the value of your estate, he or she must file a tax return for your estate, called the fiduciary return, with the IRS and make the necessary payments, if there are any.

There is a deadline for paying an estate tax — it cannot just be paid whenever your executor gets around to it. That deadline is regularly nine months after the date of death, but sometimes arrangements can be made for special circumstances.

If your estate is worth less than $1.5 million, you will not have to worry about federal estate tax, but you might still be looking at state estate taxes in some states. The best way to avoid taxes is to leave your entire estate to your spouse, a charity, or some combination thereof.

Your executor has a few options for saving some tax money, but this is where advice from an estate professional is crucial. If your executor does the wrong thing, it will cost him personally. Your executor should consider the following:

- Be sure all possible deductions are included in the fiduciary return; these include funeral expenses, expenses to your estate (e.g., appraisal fees or probate court costs), debts (e.g., mortgage or credit cards), charitable contributions, and marital deductions. The marital deduction can only be taken if your spouse is a U.S. citizen.

- Value the assets of the estate at a later date as opposed to right at death. This can only be done under the correct circumstances, and whether it is a beneficial move depends upon the individual estate and time of death.
- Income going into the estate can be manipulated to the advantage of the estate. Timing the sale of property or sending out requests for payments due can be scheduled to the advantage of filing the deceased's last income tax return and the fiduciary return the executor must file for the estate.
- Estate distributions to beneficiaries can also be timed so that the beneficiary must pay the tax, not the estate: If the payments to beneficiaries are made before the fiduciary return is filed, then the estate's value drops, making the taxes due also drop.

Your beneficiaries can also reduce their tax bills by declining to accept a bequest. Federal and state tax laws permit a disclaimer, which is a refusal to accept a gift. Whether this is a single beneficiary or joint bequest, one or both parties can decline, but it must be refused in writing, commonly within nine months of your death.

There are choices you can make in your estate planning before others need to make decisions about how to handle the taxes on your estate. When properly coordinated, some choices create an opportunity to reduce the potential tax burden on your estate and beneficiaries. These are some ways to reduce taxes, so it is a good idea to keep these in the back of your mind while working on your complete estate plan:

- Make gifts before you die to reduce your estate's value.
- Put property into tax-free trusts. *See Chapter 6 for more information about your choices.*
- Schedule property transfers to take place at the time of your death.

- Coordinate your estate planning with your spouse and divvy up assets to the best advantage for both of you.
- Use permissible exemptions, such as leaving your entire estate to your spouse.
- Consider investing in life insurance and structuring the policies carefully. *See Chapter 7 for more information on how this works.*

But like all estate planning decisions, choosing the wrong options or not using the right language can lay waste to all your careful planning. Do not try this on your own.

• Did You Know? •

The fees paid to an executor as compensation for the time he or she puts into managing and closing out your estate are taxable income. If your executor opts not to accept a fee, then the money you designate for that purpose becomes part of your estate. If it is not held in a tax-free account, that money can be subject to estate tax.

☑ Watch Out for This!

☐ Talk to your executor about a fee. If she does not want to be compensated, then you can plan accordingly.

CASE STUDY: TAX ADVICE FROM THE IRS

Internal Revenue Service (IRS)
1-800-829-1040
Hours of Operation: Monday - Friday, 7 a.m. - 10 p.m. your local time (Alaska & Hawaii follow Pacific Time)
www.irs.gov

The IRS is the ultimate source for all things related to taxation. Its website offers extensive resources for those who wish to learn more about anything related to taxes. What follows is a copy of the Frequently Asked Questions (FAQ) on the Estate Taxes page. The IRS is not in the habit of helping people figure out how to reduce their tax bills, but they will give you all you need to know to be "legal." Simply achieving the goal of compliance with tax law is not something even the FAQ can guarantee. The recurring qualifiers and other sources you need to check make it clear that dealing with estate taxes on your own is risky.

When can I expect the Estate Tax Closing Letter?

There can be some variation, but for returns that are accepted as filed and contain no other errors or special circumstances, you should expect to wait about four to six months after the return is filed to receive your closing letter. Returns that are selected for examination or reviewed for statistical purposes will take longer.

What is included in the estate?

The gross estate of the decedent consists of an accounting of everything you own or have certain interests in at the date of death. The fair market value of these items is used, not necessarily what you paid for them or what their values were when you acquired them. The total of all of these items is your gross estate. The includible property may consist of cash and securities, real estate, insurance, trusts, annuities, business interests and other assets. Keep in mind that the gross estate will likely include non-probate as well as probate property.

I own a ½ interest in a farm (or building or business) with my brother (sister, friend, other). What is included?

Depending on how your ½ interest is held and treated under state law, and how it was acquired, you would probably only include ½ of its value in your gross estate. However, many other factors influence this answer, so you would need to visit with a tax or legal professional to make that determination.

What is excluded from the estate?

Generally, the gross estate does not include property owned solely by the decedent's spouse or other individuals. Lifetime gifts that are complete (no powers or other control over the gifts are retained) are not included in the gross estate (but taxable gifts are used in the computation of the estate tax). Life estates given to the decedent by others in which the decedent has no further control or power at the date of death are not included.

What deductions are available to reduce the estate tax?

1. Marital deduction: One of the primary deductions for married decedents is the marital deduction. All property that is included in the gross estate and passes to the surviving spouse is eligible for the marital deduction. The property must pass "outright." In some cases, certain life estates also qualify for the marital deduction.
2. Charitable deduction: If the decedent leaves property to a qualifying charity, it is deductible from the gross estate.
3. Mortgages and debt
4. Administration expenses of the estate
5. Losses during estate administration

What other information do I need to include with the return?

Among other items listed:

1. Copies of the death certificate
2. Copies of the decedent's will and/or relevant trusts
3. Copies of appraisals
4. Copies of relevant documents regarding litigation involving the estate
5. Documentation of any unusual items shown on the return (partially included assets, losses, near date of death transfers, others)

What is "fair market value?"

Fair market value is defined as "the price at which the property would change hands between a willing buyer and a willing seller, neither being under any compulsion to buy or to sell and both having reasonable knowledge of relevant facts. The fair market value of a particular item of property includible in the decedent's gross estate is not to be determined by a forced sale price. Nor is the fair market value of an item of property to be determined by the sale price of the item in a market other than that in which such item is most commonly sold to the public, taking into account the location of the item wherever appropriate."

What about the value of my family business/farm?

Generally, the fair market value of such interests owned by the decedent are includible in the gross estate at date of death. However, for certain farms or businesses operated as a family farm or business, reductions to these amounts may be available.

In the case of a qualifying family farm, IRC §2032A allows a reduction from value of up to $1,000,000.

A similar deduction for a qualifying family-owned business (IRC §2057) was revoked beginning in 2004.

What if I do not have everything ready for filing by the due date?

The estate's representative may request an extension of time to file for up to six months from the due date of the return. However, the correct amount of tax is still due by the due date, and interest is accrued on any amounts still owed by the due date that are not paid at that time.

Whom should I hire to represent me and prepare and file the return?

The Internal Revenue Service cannot make recommendations about specific individuals, but there are several factors to consider:

1. How complex is the estate? By the time most estates reach $1,000,000, there is usually some complexity involved.
2. How large is the estate?
3. In what condition are the decedent's records?
4. How many beneficiaries are there, and are they cooperative?
5. Do I need an attorney, CPA, enrolled agent (EA), or other professional(s)?

With these questions in mind, it is a good idea to discuss the matter with several attorneys and CPAs or EAs. Ask about how much experience they have had and ask for referrals. This process should be similar to locating a good physician. Locate other individuals who have had similar experiences and ask for recommendations.

Finally, after the individual(s) are employed and begin to work on estate matters, make sure the lines of communication remain open so that there are no surprises during administration or if the estate tax return is examined.

Finally, most estates engage the services of both attorneys and CPAs or EAs. The attorney usually handles probate matters and reviews the impact of documents on the estate tax return. The CPA or EA often handles the actual return preparation and some representation of the estate in matters with the IRS. However, some attorneys handle all of the work. CPAs and EAs may also handle most of the work, but cannot take care of probate matters and other situations where a law license is required. In addition, other professionals (such as appraisers, surveyors, financial advisers, and others) may need to be engaged during this time.

Do I have to talk to the IRS during an examination?

You do not have to be present during an examination unless an IRS representative needs to ask specific questions. Although you may represent yourself during an examination, most executors prefer that professional(s) they have employed handle this phase of administration. They may delegate authority for this by signing a designation on the Form 706 itself, or executing Form 2848 Power of Attorney.

What if I disagree with the examination proposals?

You have many rights and avenues of appeal if you disagree with any proposals made by the IRS.

What happens if I sell property that I have inherited?

The sale of such property is usually considered the sale of a capital asset and may be subject to capital gains (or loss) treatment. However, IRC §1014 provides that the basis of property acquired from a decedent is its fair market value at the date of death, so there is usually little or no gain to account for if the sale occurs soon after the date of death. (Remember, the rules are different for determining the basis of property received as a lifetime gift).

Death is Big Business

The U.S. federal government is the first beneficiary to get a share of your estate, or any estate in the union. The IRS creates numerous statistics for everything they do, including tracking the number of deaths by state, the number of estates that pay taxes, and the amount of taxes paid. Part of that information is listed below to give you a sense of just how much money was added to the coffers of the U.S. government.

These numbers are in the thousands of dollars. After you add the zeros, you might find a new source of motivation for doing your planning now so your family does not have to pay later.

Statistic of income (SOI) estate tax data tables, selected years of death

The data included in these SOI tables are for returns filed for decedents who died in the same year and whose estates would have been subject to the same tax law and similar economic conditions.

Estate tax returns filed for 2004 decedents, by state of residence

[All figures are estimates based on a sample — money amounts are in thousands of dollars.]

State of residence	Gross estate, tax purposes [1]		Net estate tax	
Total	**42,239**	**185,921,379**	**19,294**	**22,219,722**
Alabama	409	1,582,888	186	192,473
Alaska	31	99,483	* 4	* 3,739
Arizona	621	2,408,320	302	311,565
Arkansas	265	974,431	108	117,256
California	8,464	34,208,317	3,782	4,131,248
Colorado	529	1,630,180	232	143,801
Connecticut	783	3,884,353	341	598,826
Delaware	223	721,092	136	87,531
District of Columbia	177	838,357	95	83,900

State of residence	Gross estate, tax purposes [1]		Net estate tax	
Georgia	900	4,077,616	322	405,561
Florida	4,090	20,245,897	1,871	2,635,096
Hawaii	164	677,400	64	61,901
Idaho	109	523,850	40	50,694
Illinois	1,957	8,149,220	999	946,912
Indiana	650	2,831,953	311	317,585
Iowa	474	1,425,778	184	158,665
Kansas	460	1,363,923	178	103,960
Kentucky	329	1,130,537	142	146,137
Louisiana	347	2,018,730	151	147,549
Maine	168	659,868	75	91,739
Maryland	1,065	4,307,335	550	482,638
Massachusetts	1,351	5,074,541	687	604,858
Michigan	951	8,439,720	380	1,217,440
Minnesota	575	2,875,632	203	489,367
Mississippi	188	803,735	97	126,962
Missouri	809	3,273,612	379	431,486
Montana	142	387,347	59	20,450
Nebraska	292	3,864,505	153	238,470
Nevada	300	1,523,564	164	211,414
New Hampshire	207	682,735	102	94,771
New Jersey	1,528	5,845,773	719	583,693
New Mexico	200	581,845	96	68,503
New York	3,156	17,657,621	1,539	2,425,496
North Carolina	970	3,709,205	430	409,190
North Dakota	45	233,142	* 18	* 12,693
Ohio	1,360	5,276,026	552	457,293
Oklahoma	320	1,146,682	173	147,687
Oregon	306	1,271,623	156	117,853
Pennsylvania	1,497	6,044,429	641	618,191
Rhode Island	197	675,120	69	69,145
South Carolina	285	1,429,461	131	126,410
South Dakota	113	559,505	* 21	* 8,229
Tennessee	519	1,907,851	228	206,705
Texas	1,708	7,601,993	833	1,021,141
Utah	136	582,465	43	68,946

State of residence	Gross estate, tax purposes [1]		Net estate tax	
Vermont	94	606,845	33	87,589
Virginia	1,149	4,106,031	507	470,479
Washington	720	2,527,374	294	275,636
West Virginia	171	485,637	106	53,936
Wisconsin	592	2,332,999	309	248,192
Wyoming	62	220,794	41	23,807
Other areas [2]	81	434,037	58	64,917

NOTE: Detail may not add to total because of rounding.

** Estimates should be used with caution because of the small number of sample returns on which they were based.*

[1] Gross estate is shown at the value used to determine estate tax liability. The value could be determined as of the decedent's date of death or six months thereafter (i.e., alternate valuation method).

[2] Includes U.S. territories, U.S. citizens domiciled abroad, and a small number of returns for whom state of residence was unknown.

CHAPTER 5

Wills

A family, dressed head to toe in black, sitting around grandpa's book-lined study, fidgets while the elderly lawyer sitting behind the leather-topped desk cleans his glasses and clears his throat before rasping, "Being of sound mind and body…" The scene is pure Hollywood, but most lawyers will tell you to save the drama for personal letters and keep your will legally correct to avoid potential problems. Make sure beneficiaries know what they are getting so that the day after the funeral, your family can be at home and not in a lawyer's office getting tied up in more drama.

A will is a legal document in which you identify what people or institutions receive money and property from your estate after your death. It also serves to appoint guardianship of children or adults who are your legal responsibility and designates, as well as an executor to manage your estate after you die. With standard will forms available on the Internet, it would seem that preparing a will is easy. But choosing the wrong kind of will, not having enough witnesses, leaving out key language required by Michigan, or inadequate particulars can mean the state, not you, will decide what happens to your estate.

There are things called will substitutes, such as a living trust, that can accomplish many of the things a will is designed to do, but it is still a good idea to have a will in addition to your other estate-planning options. That is because the state imposes a will on you if you do not write one of your own. If you die leaving possessions behind, someone has to divvy them up; the state assumes that responsibility if you do not do a good job of it.

When you die, if you have a valid will, you die "testate." If you do not have a will when you die, then you are "intestate," and there are laws in Michigan that determine what happens to your belongings. The legal system will distribute your assets, not you. Because your debts have to be paid when you die, including federal and state taxes, your creditors get paid first, and then your beneficiaries will get what is left over.

Most experts will tell you that, for the relatively low cost of having a will prepared by a lawyer, the safety and protection it provides are worth the investment of time and money. But before you can ask about one, you need to know what goes into a will.

Will Basics

To make sure your will is legal and can be executed, some essential information is necessary. Using your legal name in your will, the one that is on your birth certificate and under which you file your tax returns, makes it harder for someone to challenge your will — be that the state, a person, or an institution.

Michigan will have jurisdiction over your will if you are a resident of the state. That means, after you die, your will is submitted to probate court. The address listed in your will ought to be the state in which you vote, hold a driver's license, and have your primary residence. Documentation is necessary to prove the state in which you live.

One more state-related issue is ownership of property outside Michigan. If you live in Michigan but own a condo in another state, the out-of-state property will not be handled by the Michigan probate court. The court in the state where the property is located will oversee the transition of ownership. When preparing your will, you need to consider this. Just because you own it does not mean you get to control what happens to it after your death.

Wills Defined

The will that most people think of, called a simple will, is a legal document that applies to only one person. But all wills, to be legal, need to include a number of elements. The will needs to identify who you are, your beneficiaries, your executor, the directions you leave for the care of people for whom you are responsible, and the distribution of your assets.

Every will needs to have these basic elements:

- **Beneficiary:** The individual(s) or group(s) that will receive the property
- **Executor:** Also called a personal representative, the individual who handles the property you are leaving behind. If you die without a will, the court appoints an administrator, frequently a spouse or adult child, who will serve in the same capacity of handling all the paperwork, preparing of assets, dealing with likely heirs, handling claims from creditors, making payments on outstanding debt, and other estate-related matters.
- **Clauses:** The sections in your will that likely organize the information in a specific order
    - ***Opening clauses:*** Lay out the basic information about who you are and set the stage for the clauses that follow:
        - Introductory clause identifies you as the person who is making the will.
        - Family-statement clause introduces and identifies the family members who will be referred to later in the will.

- ▸ Tax clause explains how the taxes of your estate will be paid.

- ***Survival clause:*** This leaves everything in your estate to one named person. Married people frequently do this to ensure that everything goes to the surviving spouse.

- ***Guardianship clause:*** The appointment of a guardian for minor children (under the age of 18); a successor guardian should also be named as a backup.

- ***Giving clauses:*** These clauses leave specific bequests — property that is identified by name and description — to beneficiaries and explain what property goes to which person and under what circumstances. These can be as broad or explicit as you want. They are divided up according to the following categories:

  - ▸ *Real property clauses:* Statements that match up property with a person. For example: You want your spouse, Susan, to have the house and your brother, Fred, to have your antique baseball card collection.

  - ▸ *Personal property clauses:* Used when you want to be explicit in your instructions. For example: You want Teddy to get the Google stock, and Elizabeth gets the General Motors stock.

- ***Residuary clause, or residue:*** Addresses the "leftovers," the balance of your estate that you do not single out in detail in a specific clause. The residuary clause is essential for any kind of will to make sure that anything you forget or might have acquired after the will was prepared can be distributed. Naming at least one beneficiary is a good idea to keep your assets out of the hands of the courts; naming two or more alternative beneficiaries is better. For example: You want Bertha Jones, your second cousin twice removed, and her husband, Bubba Jones, to benefit from what is not given to anyone else. If either or both of them predecease you, then all of the balance of your estate goes to Bubba Jones Jr.

- *Appointment clause:* Identifies the person who will manage your estate. For example: Robert Anthony, your best friend since college, will serve as the executor of your estate.

- *Fiduciary powers clause:* The language that gives your executor the power to serve as your executor, including any duties that go beyond the basic requirements in Michigan regulations. For example: Robert Anthony will have the ability to provide your spouse, children, and/or parents with income until your estate is settled.

- *Ending clauses:* These include the legalities to meet statutory requirements so that your will is legal and valid, which include (but are not limited to) your signature, date, location of the signing, and witnesses.

Your will can be as broad or specific as you choose. As one piece of your overall estate plan, your will should be seen as one of several tools and prepared accordingly.

If you want to keep your affairs private, then a broader will would be in order. Once a will is entered in Michigan probate court, anyone can read it because it becomes a public record. If you have seen the children of a deceased friend get into fistfights over a raggedy old couch or go to court over an off-shore investment account, you might want to go into more detail.

There are different kinds of wills from which to choose to meet your specific needs. The format of these wills changes depending on who is represented in the will, what the will is designed to do, or how it is prepared.

Tips for Creating Your Will

Essentials elements for a valid will include:

- **Being in written form.** Wills that are given verbally rarely stand up in court and only on a limited basis where allowed.
- **Your name and age**
- **"Being of sound mind."** This means you know the property in your possession and the people or institutions identified as beneficiaries.
- **Clear statement and intention to transfer property**
- **Signed voluntarily** in the presence of two competent witnesses
- **Witnessed properly.** Two competent adults are all that is needed. Note that in Georgia, the witnesses can be named as beneficiaries, but being a witness to the will voids the gift bequeathed in the will.
- **Executed properly.** The will must include a statement that attests to the fact that this is your will, the date, the place it is signed, and that it is signed in front of witnesses.

Mistakes to avoid in your will include:

- Making dramatic personal statements that have nothing to do with the distribution of property, which can end up creating confusion.
- Not being specific enough — if language is ambiguous, it is subject to interpretation, and the court makes the final ruling.
- Not asking someone to be your executor or take power-of-attorney responsibilities.
- "Leftover" and "not enough" property to meet the conditions of your will.

- Using beneficiaries as witnesses who sign the will. You want to avoid the potential appearance of a conflict of interest or having undue influence over the person making the will.
- Making many changes at once or over time and not creating a new will; excessive changes can lead to confusion.

A few more things...

The original document

If the original will is stored in a safe deposit box, it could become inaccessible after your death if that box is in your name only. Have your lawyer retain the original will in his or her files so that it is readily accessible.

Other will-related documents

Your original durable power of attorney, medical power of attorney, living will, and any other documents related to incapacitation should also be stored in your lawyer's office. Those taking responsibility for making medical, financial, or other decisions ought to have a copy of that power of attorney.

Copies

Choosing to keep your will private is a decision you will need to make based on a conversation with your lawyer. Unusual clauses or issues might warrant making copies of the documents and sharing them with key people in advance so that nobody is surprised when the will is executed. Your wishes regarding what should happen if you were to become incapacitated and who is responsible for making decisions on your behalf ought to be shared with all family members and close friends. This way, there can be no question about what you would like done.

**Note: Do not sign copies of a will, or it might qualify as a legal "duplicate original." Write "COPY" in ink on each page just to make sure nobody can claim a copy is the original.

Especially in the case of serious illness and a "do not resuscitate" (DNR) order, a living will, and organ donation, your physicians and other medical providers need to have copies. Your doctors might have their own form for you to fill out related to these matters; be sure to check.

The "who" of a will

Mutual will: A plan for your estate prepared in conjunction with another person

For example: Sisters Carol and Angie agree to support their disabled brother, Brian, and Grandma Jane. So, they decide that no matter who dies first, 40 percent of either estate goes to Brian, 40 percent goes to Grandma Jane, and the remaining 20 percent goes to other beneficiaries. When the other person dies, 50 percent of her estate goes to Brian, 20 percent goes to Grandma Jane, and the remaining 30 percent goes to other beneficiaries. If Grandma Jane dies before Carol or Angie, her portion goes to Brian.

Joint will: One legal document for any two people, such as you and your spouse. The problem with this kind of will is that it is irrevocable, which means it cannot be changed after one of the two parties dies. The reason is that all decisions must be made by both people. A lawyer can tell you when this kind of will is a good idea, but most suggest separate wills to avoid complications.

Simple will: A single legal document that is written by one person which identifies who you are, your beneficiaries, your executor, the directions you leave for the care of people for whom you are responsible, and the distribution of your assets.

The "what" of a will

Pour-over will: This will place some property into a trust that was established while you were still alive.

Testamentary trust will: This will move your assets into one or more trusts after your death. *See Chapter 6 for more information on trusts.*

The "how" of a will

Holographic will: A handwritten document that is signed by you but not witnessed by anyone else. Some states, such as Michigan, recognize a handwritten will as valid. *See Chapter 11 for more information on how this works in Michigan.*

Nuncupative will: Also called an oral will, this is a spoken will. Some states only allow this kind of will if someone is literally on his or her deathbed, and it only covers personal property of little or no value. Michigan does not recognize nuncupative wills.

Video will: In most cases, a will recorded on a videotape or digital video device (DVD) will not be accepted as a legal document. Video wills are not recognized in Michigan. Some states will, in extreme circumstances, allow a will to be recorded by a terminally ill person from a deathbed — literally. Recording messages to loved ones might be something you want to do, but it is better to prepare legal documents, such as a will, with a lawyer.

It is important to consider how the will you prepare will complement or conflict with the other elements of your estate plan.

• *Did You Know?* •

"Non-traditional" children are becoming as common as the "traditional" kind — the biological offspring of a heterosexual couple. Even though some of those biologics are considered "illegitimate" when their parents are not legally married, federal and state law typically defines "children" in that traditional sense.

Over time, legally adopted children have become synonymous with biological children in the eyes of the law. But in an era when divorce, infertility, and same-sex couples mean kids become part of a family though in vitro fertilization (IVF), adoptions originating in a foreign country, and stepchildren, inheritance can be a tricky thing.

A child born outside a legally recognized union — in most states, including Michigan, this is defined as a marriage between a woman and a man — will automatically inherit her/his mother's estate. An inheritance from the biological father is not necessarily automatic.

Many state laws allow a child to inherit from a man who is identified as the father through a paternity test. The father can also marry the mother after the child is born and acknowledge himself as the father of the "out of wedlock" daughter/son. If paternity — the action taken to establish the biological relationship of an adult in a parent-child relationship — is not established, then a child cannot inherit from the estate of the unidentified parent.

☑ Watch Out for This!

- ☐ You must legally adopt stepchildren for them to be considered part of your family; if you do not adopt them and your will directs your estate to fund trust funds for "my children," only those minors who are recognized by the state – not you – as yours will be able to receive a bequest.
- ☐ A paternity test is the comparison of blood taken from the potential father against a blood sample of the child.
- ☐ A paternity suit is a legal action that is initiated to establish a man as the biological father of a child.
- ☐ While the question of paternity is typically associated with the father, a biological parental test can be used to establish the biological relationship of a mother as well, in the case of abandonment or other circumstances in which a mother is not clearly identified.

The "Other" Will

Many people prepare a living will at the time they draw up the will for their estate, even though it has nothing to do with your house, car, or checking account. A living will or medical directive is a document in which you spell out the decisions you have made about your medical care while you are still alive. The idea is to decide what kind of measures you want — or do not want — taken on your behalf if you should become incapacitated.

All states now recognize some mechanism equivalent or similar to a living will, but the documents are not uniform. Some states will only allow living wills to apply to a person who is permanently unconscious or has a terminal illness. Others will allow them for advanced-stage illnesses, such as the final stages of Alzheimer's, when death is not imminent. Michigan does not expressly acknowledge a living will, but does recognize the concept of advance directive through appointment of someone to make decisions under a durable power of attorney for health care if you become incompetent to speak for yourself. *This is further addressed for Michigan in Chapter 11.*

Wording for living wills is essential. A statement such as "I do not want to become a burden to my family" is vague. Your living will should be specific and address your medical history, so consulting your doctor about what-if scenarios is essential to understanding what kinds of life-saving measures might be taken to keep you alive. If you have a history of congestive heart failure in your family and have been diagnosed with the same condition, but do not want extraordinary measures, such as being kept alive by feeding tube or respirator, taken to prolong your life, your wish needs to be spelled out.

Another way to make sure your wishes are followed regarding your medical care is to designate a health care power of attorney (HCPA), also known as a medical power of attorney. Your HCPA involves designating a person to make medical decisions for you when you cannot do it for yourself by signing a legal document known as a power of attorney. Many states have laws that allow family members to make some or all of your health care decisions. These family consent or health surrogate laws follow a specific order of kinship for who makes a decision; if you are married, your spouse, not your sister, will be your surrogate. Even though the default position of most physicians is to consult the family, having your wishes spelled out in an HCPA relieves your family of having to deal with that issue.

A durable power of attorney can also be used to give someone else the authority to make medical decisions on your behalf. This kind of power of attorney allows an authorized person to act on behalf of the grantor of that power of attorney.

Making decisions about life-sustaining treatment, artificial nutrition and hydration, and organ donation are the advanced directives most people prepare. A DNR order — do not resuscitate if you appear to have died — is an example of the kind of decision you can make and communicate in your living will. Michigan allows directives for DNR and organ donations. Completing an organ donor card will reinforce your decision to make that gift, if that is important to you.

To avoid confusion or conflict at a later date, make sure your living will is properly executed with witnesses present. Then make sure close family members and friends have copies of the document and understand your wishes. That way, when a medical decision needs to be made, there is not any question about what you would want.

• *Did You Know?* •

The Health Insurance Portability and Accountability Act (HIPAA) is a federal law passed in 1996 that did more than just create more forms for you to sign when you go to the doctor's office. It protects medical insurance coverage for employees when they change or lose their jobs. It also forced the creation and implementation of national standards for conducting electronic medical care transactions for providers, medical insurance companies/plans, and employers. But it also put into place privacy protections that prevent caregivers from sharing your personal information with anyone not explicitly authorized by you.

Questions were raised about the access to private information for someone holding a health care/medical power of attorney: Can that person be given confidential medical information by medical staff in order to make informed decisions, as the incapacitated person expected?

The answer is yes. A form explicitly giving your designated person access to your information is not necessary. The U.S. Department of Health and Human

Services confirmed that the power of attorney supersedes the HIPAA privacy requirements.

It is still a good idea to make sure all your medical care providers — primary care physician, eye doctor, dentist, and any specialists — have a copy of your health care/medical power of attorney on file. This can help avoid delays in case of an emergency.

People Speaking for You

After you are no longer able to speak for yourself, others will speak on your behalf. Those individuals you choose to act for you have a host of legal and moral issues to manage, so choosing who will represent you is a serious matter. The lawyer preparing your will and the executor of your will are the two people who will have the most immediate and significant impact on what happens after you are gone. To choose the best people for these tasks, it is important to know what they do.

Wills attorney

The lawyer you work with to draw up your will needs to know what he or she is doing. In addition to being well versed in federal law regarding estates, he or she also needs to know what Michigan requires and what makes a will valid/legal. If your estate plan includes several planning professionals, such as a CPA or financial planner, then your lawyer needs to be someone who can work well with others.

The more elusive criteria for choosing your legal representative are those things that give you a sense that you can trust and work with this person. You need to be able to share all the details of your estate and wishes so that he or she will be able to give you the best advice. You also need to be comfortable going back repeatedly to make changes to your will that reflect the changes in your life.

It is equally important to be able to communicate comfortably and effectively with the person who will manage your estate.

Executor

After you are gone, you want someone to take care of your estate the way you would. That means finding the right person or company to handle the things that need to be done after you die. Regardless of the individual(s) you select, there are things that this person must do:

- Guide your will through the probate process to make sure it is accepted as valid. This also means defending the will against any contest challenges.
- Collect your assets.
- Oversee the transition of gifts made to beneficiaries. This might include a title transfer for a house or making sure a life insurance policy check is made out in the correct name.
- Review, evaluate, and pay any claims against your estate. These include taxes and outstanding bills that are owed.
- Raise the money to pay claims. This can mean selling assets, such as a house or car.
- Prepare and file an accounting of all financial transactions for the court.

Failure to do any of these things can have serious consequences for the executor, so it is extremely important that the person who agrees to take on this responsibility knows what is expected.

Because this is such a time-consuming, key responsibility, you do have the option to pay your executor a fee for his or her services. Whether to do this is a decision to discuss with your lawyer.

While it is impossible to predict how someone will handle this kind of responsibility, giving careful thought to who will carry out your wishes is important.

Change and Your Will

Simply put, things happen. That is why it is essential to make sure that changes you experience in your life are reflected in your will. Once a will is written, it is not etched in stone — it can be revised or even replaced.

To make a change to a specific portion of your will, you create a codicil, a separate legal document that adds to your existing will. It is an easy way to make a few simple changes. When you are older, a codicil is an easy way to protect your will from being challenged due to incompetence. If you only change one part, then the codicil might be successfully challenged, but not the majority of your will.

You might wind up changing your will without even realizing it. If you bequest specific property to someone, such as a boat, but then you sell it or it sinks during a storm, the court will address it. No matter what the reason, if property is missing from your estate that is named in your will, then it is considered adeemed. Ademption statutes govern the distribution of your belongings, and the state will take over if items are missing. There are ways to avoid this problem, such as having "backup" property to serve as a substitute.

If a beneficiary in your will dies before you do, that creates an antilapse. If the property exists and no contingent beneficiary is named, then the state steps in if it has an antilapse statute. If your state does not have such a statute, then the property would most likely be covered by the residuary clause, but it is best to check with an attorney to be sure. Michigan has an antilapse statute.

Maybe at the time of your death you are carrying a ton of debt that you were going to pay off in the near future. An unexpected departure is something you can plan for in your will, but it takes some planning. The usual method for paying off debt is to sell property in the estate, such as jewelry, antiques, or vacation property. But if there still is not enough money to take care of those debts, your house might have to be sold, leaving your family homeless. Some states have a homestead exemption statute that protects the family home from being sold. However, it is not a 100-percent guarantee, so you need to work with your estate-planning team to figure out how to address this and other "what if" scenarios. Michigan has a limited homestead exemption of $3,500, with a covered area limitation of an acre of urban land and 40 acres of rural land.

Downtown Detroit Skyline and Detroit River, Michigan

CHAPTER 6

Trusts

The image many people have of a child with a trust fund is someone with access to all the money necessary to pay for a college education, an extended tour of Europe, or a carefree future without money problems. The truth of the matter is that you do not have to be independently wealthy to set up a trust, and their uses are significantly more diverse than the aforementioned stereotype.

The basic idea behind a trust is to set aside specific property for specific people or institutions so that you, not the courts, decide what will happen to your estate. Knowing what you want to put into the trust, who benefits from the trust, and the price to be paid — set-up fees, taxes, time — is essential to making sure you choose the right trust.

There are at least a dozen different kinds of trusts with various combinations of legal and tax implications, so there is no such thing as a "standard" trust. A book like this one can help you learn what a trust is, but any "one-size-fits-all" trust template is a disaster waiting to happen.

Each trust is customized to meet the needs of the individual — that is what makes a trust so attractive and difficult. Laws and tax requirements at the federal and state level are constantly changing, and so are your needs. With the extremely real possibility that your trust could end up in probate or the hands of the government, it is essential to work with an estate planner and lawyer to make sure you have the proper documents in place so that your trust is legal and enforceable.

To make sure the outcome you want is the one you get, learn what a trust is, its benefits, and its drawbacks. The steps to set up a trust and the elements of a trust can be easy enough to understand: Identify what property will be included, who benefits, who manages the trust, tax implications for all the people involved, and how the law governs all that activity. The tricky part is learning about the different kinds of trusts and matching them up with your wishes.

What is a Trust?

A trust is a legal arrangement that involves the transfer of property from the original owner to a person or a company for the purpose of holding and maintaining the property until it is handed over to the beneficiary — the individual or institution designated to receive the property.

It seems straightforward enough, until you get into the many legal terms, people, laws, and taxes that go into the creation of a trust. With many interchangeable terms, some of which are as confusing as the Greek or Roman terms from which they originated, a list of who is who and what is what is helpful. The following situation will assist you with recognizing the roles each person plays in a trust.

People: Aunt Tara wants to set up a trust for her house so that her niece Betsy will have a place to set up her veterinary clinic after she finishes her education. But she does not know when Betsy will graduate, so she wants her grandson Charles to take care of the place if she — Aunt Tara — dies. In case something happens to Charles, his wife Kim will take on that responsibility.

- **Trustor *(Aunt Tara):*** The person who sets up the trust. Other names commonly used are creator, donor, settlor, or grantor.

- **Beneficiary *(Betsy):*** The individual(s) or group(s) that will receive the property in the trust. This can be a single person, a group of people, one group, several groups, or a combination of any of these.

- **Trustee *(Charles):*** The person or company that will oversee or manage the trust once it is established. This person (or group) will make sure the property in the trust is safe and in good order until it is turned over to the beneficiary. This includes paying any taxes, performing repairs, or anything else an owner would do. The trustee is obligated to carry out the terms of the trust and can be paid for this effort, if terms for this are included in the trust language.

- **Successor trustee *(Kim):*** Someone who will step in if the primary trustee is unable to serve or cannot continue to manage your trust. This person will have the same legal obligations for managing the trust as the original trustee, should the successor assume the management responsibilities.

The individual or company designated to serve as trustee carries a significant amount of responsibility and needs to be someone you trust implicitly. The potential for a conflict of interest or being swayed by the temptation to do something inappropriate, such as stealing from the trust or neglecting the work, needs to be considered. Putting language in the trust documents that spells out the responsibilities of the trustees is essential, and creating a mechanism of oversight and removal will prevent your heirs from losing what is supposed to be theirs.

Things and strings: Aunt Tara's house sits on four acres of land with an outbuilding to store the lawn tractor and other equipment. Over the years, she sold off the other 12 acres, so she invested the money in a mutual fund. Aunt Tara had her lawyer set up a trust fund that gives Betsy the interest from the mutual fund to pay tuition when it is due in the fall, but Aunt Tara's mutual fund will not go to Betsy until she graduates from college. The house in the care of Charles will also go to Betsy after she graduates.

- **Property:** Anything you want to give to other people, also referred to as principal. There are all kinds of legal terms for the "stuff" you own, and you have to make sure you use the right words to identify everything from money in a safe or checking account to a rocking chair or commemorative baseball. This can be real property or real estate (ten-acre farm), tangible personal property (the things you can touch, such as a lawn tractor and other equipment), or intangible personal property (financial assets such as certificates of deposit).

- **Trust agreement:** The legal document that spells out the terms of a trust, including the people and conditions and the rules that must be followed. Some are state or federal laws, and others are specific conditions. (Trust fund)

- **Funding a trust:** The placement of property in a trust; that same property will be called trust principal once it is under the auspices of the trust agreement.

- **Provisions:** The clauses that spell out how you want your wishes carried out. Distribution provisions will identify who will receive the income and the frequency of those distributions (pay tuition when it is due in the fall). Special provisions encompass all requirements that are unique to the beneficiary or the assets. (Graduates from college)

- **Legal title:** This gives the trustee ownership of the property in the trust for the duration of the trustee's responsibility. (House in Charles's care)

- **Beneficial title:** Also known as equitable title, this is the right of the person or institution to take possession of or benefit from the property in the trust. (Goes to Betsy)

The plan can be incredibly clear, but whether the result matches that plan depends on the kind of trust you choose, the way the documents are worded, and the way the people involved carry out their tasks. It is easier to make mistakes than it is to get it right, and those mistakes can be costly for loved ones. If you are not careful, they can inherit a big mess instead of the things you want them to have.

One way to avoid such a mess is to carefully choose a trustee who will carry out your wishes and do so legally. Being a trustee is more than just whipping out a checkbook and signing a few papers now and then.

Talking to Your Estate Planner about Trusts

Before you sit down with your estate planner, take some time to think about the questions you have regarding your life circumstances. Here are a few questions to keep in mind:

- What are the tax consequences for this trust? What about capital gains?
- What happens to the "leftovers" in a trust — cash, property, and everything else?
- Will there be a problem if the trust beneficiary dies before you do?
- What happens if the terms of a trust are not met — i.e., Bobby quits school before his educational trust is spent?
- When does a specific use trust terminate? For example, if Aunt Mimi's disability trust is still in place after she dies.
- What happens to an irrevocable trust if the situation changes?
- What are the advantages and disadvantages for a single person in setting up a trust?
- What happens if some of the property in your trust is community property, and you divorce?

- If you end up divorced, what happens to the education trust fund that Mom and Dad are funding for little Suzy?

Things to consider...

An estate planner can also help you address some of the unexpected or unusual life circumstances that might not be on your mind. There are also legal ramifications for your death that might not come up during your life. For example, unmarried partners do not get the same automatic consideration that a legally married couple has. A QTIP trust is not an option for a couple that does not have a legally documented marriage.

Some other things that affect the legality and terms of a trust include:

- Foreign-born spouse
- Non-biological "family" members
- Same-sex couples
- Living together — as opposed to a formal or common-law marriage
- Adoption
- Pets
- Divorce
- Multiple marriages — offspring and spouses
- Incapacitation
- Medical condition/serious illness
- Permanent disability
- Natural disaster affecting property
- Stock/real estate market crash

Types of Trusts

A trust can be set up to take effect while you are alive (inter vivos), or it can take effect after you die (testamentary). Some can be changed (revocable), and some cannot be changed no matter what (irrevocable). Some trusts can be terminated or ended, while others cannot. The purpose of a trust can result in a tax exemption or higher tax rate, depending on what the current tax law allows.

There are trusts for yourself and trusts for other people, and many of the reasons for setting up either kind are the same — tax benefits, staying out of probate court, protecting assets from creditors, or making sure money is available "just in case" for things like education, severe illness, or a disability. Considering all life's possibilities to decide which trust(s) would be helpful is a daunting task. Another way to look at the situation is to consider the kinds of trusts that already exist and have defined legal and tax consequences.

Trusts fall into a number of categories that can be described by different criteria. One criterion is the beneficiary. A marital-dedication trust is specific to the surviving, legal spouse of the deceased. A bypass trust will transfer property to someone other than your spouse, such as a child or grandchild, but allow your spouse to still benefit from the property in the trust. Some states, including Michigan, even allow you to create a trust for your pets.

Another criterion is the reason for the trust. If you want to protect the beneficiary's property so that it is available for a specific reason when it is needed, you would use a protective trust. A discretionary trust gives the trustee the ability to distribute income and property to a variety of beneficiaries; he or she also has the option to control the distributions to a single beneficiary as he or she decides is appropriate. That offers some flexibility, as does a dynasty trust; also known as a wealth trust, it can last for several generations or be set up to never end. This kind of trust helps people with a vast amount of wealth control the distribution of that money and property over a long period. However, many states limit noncharitable trusts to 90 years. Michigan takes the approach that the trust ceases when its purpose ceases.

The over arching requirements of a trust create yet another group. A split-interest means more than one individual benefits from the trust: one person or charity would have an interest in the trust for a specific period of time, and then another person or charity receives the property that remains. A support trust requires a trustee to pay only the income and property necessary to cover the cost of education or assistance, such as health care or nursing home fees, of the beneficiaries.

Some trusts are automatically irrevocable, so you have to make sure you know what you are signing before you pick up the pen. However, many trusts can be set up as revocable or irrevocable, with a variety of conditions that put the trust into one of the categories already defined by tax law. These laws continue changing to keep up with the creative efforts to avoid taxes.

These conditions and restrictions make it important to consult an estate planning specialist to discuss the trust options that will help you achieve your goals and understand the tax implications of your choices.

The following is a list of the different types of trusts:

- **Burial trust:** Provides the funds necessary to cover the cost of your burial or cremation arrangements. This can be a revocable trust, but after your death, it becomes irrevocable, and the trust cannot be used for anything else.

- **Charitable trust:** Offers the benefits of tax-free gifts for the donor. A charitable remainder trust gives gifts of interest income that are paid to specific beneficiaries, such as your spouse, for a specific period of time; at the end of that time period, a charity receives whatever is left in the trust. A charitable lead trust, or a front trust, gives the charity a specific gift before all other beneficiaries receive anything. These are both split-interest trusts. Split-interest trusts make distributions to both charitable and noncharitable beneficiaries, while providing tax benefits to their donor.

- **Crummey trust:** An exceedingly complicated trust normally set up in conjunction with an irrevocable life insurance trust to make the payments for a life insurance policy. This kind of trust requires an estate-planning attorney.

- **Educational trust:** This is a kind of protective trust that sets aside money specifically for education-related expenses, such as tuition or training fees, books, or supplies. These trusts regularly include provisions to stop payments if the student drops out of school or flunks many classes.

- **Generation-skipping transfer trust (GSTT):** A tax-saving trust designed to benefit multiple generations after you are gone.

- **Grantor-retained trusts:** These are irrevocable and noncharitable, which means they cannot be changed and the beneficiary is not a charity. There are three common types: A grantor-retained annuity trust (GRAT) gives a fixed amount of money at predetermined times, often at regularly scheduled intervals; a grantor-retained unit trust (GRUT) pays a specific percentage to the beneficiary; and a grantor-retained incomes trust (GRIT) designates specific people to receive certain property, such as stocks or a house, but the income or use of the property stays with you until your death.

- **Living trust:** Created while you are still alive, this trust allows you to be the grantor, trustee, and beneficiary, if you choose.

- **Marital dedication trust:** Puts property into a trust that is exclusively for your spouse, who decides what happens to the property after your death.

- **Minor trust:** A way to give gifts to minors that avoids the gift tax and keeps the property safe until the minor becomes an adult and can take ownership of the trust.

- **QTIP:** A qualified terminable interest property trust is a marital deduction trust. But instead of your spouse deciding who gets the property after your death, the grantor makes that decision.

- **Spendthrift trust:** A trust that is set up for someone who will not be able to handle their own affairs, i.e., someone who is mentally incompetent or might have financial problems and needs protection from creditors. The beneficiary does not own the property in the trust, just the payments that are made from the trust.

- **Special needs trust:** A support trust for a disabled person under the age of 65 (you or anyone else), this trust makes payments on the beneficiary's behalf, as required by the state as reimbursement. After the beneficiary dies, the property in the trust is paid to other beneficiaries. This trust is designed to protect your property from seizure by the government or a creditor seeking reimbursement.

- **Supplemental needs trust:** A support trust designed to provide income to a handicapped, elderly, or disabled person to supplement their income, but is structured in a way that does not reduce or jeopardize the eligibility of that person to receive public or private benefits. This trust is designed to protect your property from seizure by the government or a creditor seeking reimbursement.

- **Testamentary trust:** Created by the terms of your will after your death

- **Totten trust**: A bank account that, upon your death, immediately passes to the named beneficiary

• *Did You Know?* •

If you have a modest estate, but you still want your minor children to inherit your property, you can use the Uniform Transfer for Minors Act (UTMA) or the Uniform Gift to Minors Act (UGMA). Most states, including Michigan, have adopted this legislation, which allows you to create a custodian account for a minor.

A custodian account, which can be in the form of a trust, allows you to deposit money or property in an account set up by a bank or a brokerage firm. You name yourself as the custodian — trustee — of the account while you are alive and name a successor to take over those responsibilities after you die. This new custodian will serve in that capacity until the child reaches 18, or 21 or 25, depending on the state law.

☑ Watch Out for This!

- ☐ Some states hand over the ownership of the account to the child when he or she turns 18, and you have no say after that. This is also Michigan's position.
- ☐ Accounts for children over the age of 13 are subject to federal income tax at the children's rate. This will most certainly be lower than your tax rate, but the implications of this need to be considered.
- ☐ If you create an UGMA or UTMA account, this can reduce the amount of court paperwork and supervision, thereby lowering estate costs.
- ☐ Even if you create this kind of account, you must still name a legal guardian for your children in your will. The legal guardian can also be custodian of this kind of account, but naming a custodian of an account is not the same as naming a legal guardian.

Pros and Cons of Forming a Trust

Trusts provide some excellent benefits, but they are not the perfect solution for everything. One benefit is that some trusts can reduce the amount of taxes that have to be paid before and after you die. But if your trust is not set up properly, it might have to pay income tax. A trust can protect your assets from your creditors or those of your beneficiaries, but only if it is set up properly.

More private than a will, which becomes public record upon your death and makes the details of your estate available to anyone who wants access, a trust can keep others out of your personal business. In many cases, a trust can help keep your estate out of probate court, and it is more difficult to contest a trust than a will. The flexibility of a trust allows you to make changes and can even help with financial issues if you become disabled during your life.

The downside is that it costs money to set up a trust, and there are numerous scams out there, both foreign and domestic. So if you are not careful, you could wind up losing the property you want to go to your loved ones and charity. There also is the possibility that your trustee will abscond with the contents of the trusts and head for a non-extradition country.

Whether trusts are worth all the hassle and potential risk is up to you — and that is why is it essential to work with estate-planning specialists when setting up any trust(s).

The Dos and Don'ts for Trusts

The following tips are things to consider when you are preparing your trust:

- Think of choosing a trust as a dry run for your estate planning. Consider all possible life scenarios and how a trust will or will not help those situations.
- When setting up a trust or trusts, do them all at once so that you can save a few dollars – with any luck – and make sure none of them conflict with the others.
- Put all trust agreements in writing.
- Make sure the proper legal language is used in every agreement.
- Clearly define the trustee responsibilities and obligations. A "passive" trust, which does not define these things, might not be recognized by a court as a trust.
- Clearly identify beneficiaries.
- Clearly define the property in the trust. "Everything in the dining room" is an example of what not to do.
- Make sure the property you put into a trust will meet the needs you identify – $100,000 to pay for a college education in the year 2100 might not be enough.

- Carefully choose a trustee who will execute your wishes, take care of all legal obligations, and is willing to take on all those duties.
- Keep an eye on the content and value of each trust over time. Fluctuating market conditions and changes in your life might leave a trust underfunded, or maybe obsolete.

Notes about other information you want to learn: ________________

____

____

____

____

State Capitol in Lansing

Laughing Whitefish Falls, Michigan

CHAPTER 7

Insurance

Insurance is one part of your estate plan, and it can be an especially effective part if you have good information and advice tailored to your needs, not those of the person pushing papers across the desk for you to sign. How you want to make that money work for you should guide your shopping and decision-making. Consider:

- **Funeral expenses:** On average, these range from $5,000 to $8,000, but can go much higher.
- **Grief money:** Supports your family during their grieving period so they do not have to rush back to work to cover the bills
- **Debts**: Cover the cost of money you owe to others so that it does not reduce the size of your estate.
- **Estate costs:** Ready cash to cover estate taxes and costs for distributing your estate and provide a stipend for your executor
- **Lost income:** Gives your family access to some of the income you would have earned
- **Education funds:** Money for school, now or in the future
- **Funding a trust:** This will add to the property in the trust and be distributed like all the other assets in that trust.

- **Taxes:** Giving money to your "probate estate" is a way to make sure your estate has enough money to cover tax payment to state and federal tax collectors.

For a rather small investment, you can provide your beneficiaries with a substantial amount of money, if you choose carefully.

When you die, the insurance company that holds your life insurance policy cuts a check to your spouse, children, or parents, but there is much more to know, including the following:

- Death benefits can be taxed.
- If the beneficiary of your policy dies before you do, the money goes into probate.
- An insurance policy that invests in the stock market might actually lose value, leaving your beneficiaries with less money.
- A serious illness can devastate the assets of your estate, which means the life insurance you wanted to support your family could end up in the hands of creditors instead.

Insurance, like most things in life, is not quite as simple as it once was — or as sales reps like to make it appear. The kind of insurance you have when you are alive can affect your estate as much as the insurance you have for after your death, so this is where the here-and-now affects the future.

Insurance, simply defined, is a method to protect the things we value most. Some insurance is mandated by law (automobile insurance), while some is considered essential (health insurance), and other kinds are considered a luxury (disability and long-term care). What kind and how much insurance any individual needs is based upon individual circumstances. If you do not have a $20 million country estate, it is not likely that you are going to need the kind of liability insurance that would protect you against a lawsuit brought by someone who stayed for the weekend and was hurt while riding a horse from your stable.

As part of your overall estate plan, insurance can accomplish some of the more conventional goals people have, such as providing cash to pay taxes so that your family does not have to sell property to settle with Uncle Sam. What is slightly more uncommon is considering the impact a permanent disability can have on the assets of your estate and how you will maintain that estate until it is passed on to someone else.

Thinking about insurance before you need it is the best way to consider the host of options and tangle of details and conditions related to each. This requires much what-if speculation on your part, but educated guesses are possible when you make time to let your imagination run free.

Insurance for Here and Now

Most insurance commercials focus on the worst-case scenario to scare you into buying peace of mind. Though horrible, these situations are exactly what you need to consider. While not fun, considering the effects of a serious illness, debilitating accident, or natural disaster can point you in the right directions for figuring out your insurance needs.

Medical insurance

Frequently referred to as health insurance by those who sell it, the insurance that covers medical costs is almost never used when you are healthy; but you always have to whip out that benefits card when you fill a prescription for strep throat, have a heart attack, or break a bone.

The first question you need to consider is whether your insurance policy will cover your bills when you truly need it to, because if your insurance does not pay, you will have to. That payment can be high enough to wipe out your savings, not to mention any other assets you have built up over time. What most people consider is the amount that is deducted from every paycheck week after week, not the tens of thousands of dollars a hospital will try to collect from you after you have hit your "maximum lifetime benefit."

Even if your family has no history of colon cancer, breast cancer, heart attack, or even high cholesterol, you can still be involved in a workplace accident or a horrible car crash that is not your fault or contract a rare virus on the only trip you ever take out of the country. Anyone who has children or knows someone who has children knows that trips to the emergency room and doctor's office are the rule, not the exception.

A simple cold going around school can land your child in an intensive care unit (ICU) with walking pneumonia. Will your insurance cover a stay in a pediatric ICU? What if your child requires hospitalization while out of state visiting relatives? Knowing the terms of your medical insurance coverage, beyond the monthly premium, is an essential part of your estate planning. A few simple things to check are:

- What is the maximum lifetime benefit per person? Per policy?
- What serious illnesses are not covered?
- How is a "pre-existing condition" defined, and can that be excluded from your coverage?
- Do you have "out-of-network" coverage? Can you purchase additional coverage if you are going to travel out of your network area? Out of the country?
- What about medical care provided outside the United States? Can you get reimbursed for those costs?
- When can you make changes to your coverage?

After you find the answers to these questions, compare the information against your family medical history. Do any of the "not covered" illnesses run in your family? Also, consider what is on the horizon for your family, such as a child going to study abroad for a year or an overweight spouse starting a new exercise program without consulting a doctor. Paying a slightly higher premium now for better coverage can prevent some devastating bills later.

A person who receives a diagnosis of cancer typically does not begin thinking about funding a family trip to Bermuda; he is thinking about extensive treatments, not being able to coach Little League, and maybe being unable to work for an extended period. Do not leave everything in the hands of your insurance agent. Preparing for these "what-if" situations is your job.

Disability insurance

A disability insurance policy will make payments to you to cover living expenses and replace your lost income as a result of your inability to hold a job. So, if you cannot work because you are sick, get hurt, or for some other reason, this insurance will replace some of your lost income. Imagine what could happen to your savings if you are stuck at home in bed, but the mortgage payment, utilities bills, and furnace repair invoices keep coming.

Your ability to leave anything for your loved ones after you are gone is largely dependent upon the work you do while you are alive. While disability insurance will not replace 100 percent of your income, it would certainly be better than nothing. The question is whether the conditions and restrictions make it a worthwhile investment for you. If you feel it is a good idea, determine what kind of disability insurance will meet your needs.

There are many different disability plans out there, but they fall into two types, short- or long-term. Short-term disability provides benefits for about three months; some plans go a little longer, but they are a temporary fix. Long-term disability can provide benefits for years but does eventually end — frequently at 65, when you become eligible for social security. The benefits are as varied as the plans available. Some things to look for include:

- **When the policy goes into effect:** Some policies do not begin to make payments until you have been out of work for a specific period; they do not make payments the moment you are disabled.
- **How payments are calculated:** Some policies replace a percentage of your income, on average ranging from 50 to 75 percent.

- **Definition of disability:** You might have to be unable to work at any job, or payments might be made if you are not able to work in your chosen profession.
- **Premium payments:** How they are calculated can depend on the percentage of income replaced — more money means a higher premium — or some other criterion.

The federal government also provides a social security disability benefit for which you might be eligible. But if you think getting only 50 percent of your income reimbursed is not enough, do not count on the government to offer a 100 percent replacement.

While short-term disability can help you through a rough time, long-term disability is going to have a direct impact on your estate plan. A serious injury not only has the potential to rack up major medical bills not covered by health insurance, it can also eliminate the possibility of future investments and jeopardize your ability to pay life insurance and other premiums.

Long-term care insurance

The difference between long-term disability and long-term care insurance is that the latter provides payments to cover the cost of medical care. In-home nursing or nursing home fees are examples of what might be covered. While this might bring to mind 89-year-old Aunt Mary who could fall and break her hip, this coverage is for any debilitating injury suffered by anyone at any age.

If you fall at work and injure your back so badly that you require surgery and months of physical therapy so you can walk again, your medical insurance might not be enough to cover the entire cost. Again, it is important to understand what the policy will and will not cover and when the payments will begin. If you max out your medical insurance, but your long-term care insurance does not kick in for a year, if ever, the assets in your estate could be in jeopardy.

Looking into all these details before you need to use your insurance is the best way to learn what you need to know. Do not leave it to your family to sort out when their primary concern ought to be figuring out how to save you from the horrible fruit cocktail "the home" is passing off as nutritious and delicious.

Homeowner's/renter's insurance

If your house is your biggest asset, then protecting it is a no-brainer. The list of possible disasters can keep homeowners up all night immediately before and after buying a house. There is nothing like a down payment and an hour's worth of signing papers to make you realize what is on the line if something goes wrong. Banks are not in the habit of saying, "Your house burned down? Well, then, let us just tear up those loan papers."

Even if you do not own a home, that lease you signed is a legally binding agreement. If you are robbed or the pipes in the apartment above add a waterfall feature to your living room, you are still going to have to pay your rent, and the antique books you wanted to give to niece Amy will not be worth the paper composing the pulp they will resemble.

Making sure you can recoup the loss of your property — both real estate and the things you have to move in boxes — is essential if your estate is to have any value after a disaster — natural or otherwise. Fire, flood, earthquake, tornadoes, snow caving in a roof, wind damage, or anything else you can think of that might possibly damage your home and its contents are the things to consider when purchasing insurance.

There are some homeowners' policies that will pay off the balance of a home mortgage, leaving the bulk of your estate to replace your income if you do not want your family to worry about money after you are gone. Before signing on that dotted line, find out the circumstances under which the policy might not pay off the mortgage. Just because you die does not mean they will pay up.

Automobile insurance

An antique or exotic car collection will warrant an automobile insurance policy with special coverage for the replacement of such a rare vehicle, as opposed to what the average driver needs. That kind of insurance is important to have if your car collection does not fit on a shelf in the family room, but for everyday driving, everyone needs some basic minimums.

If you lease a car, then you know the leasing agency requires specific limits for personal injury and liability. Michigan also requires a minimum amount of insurance coverage to legally drive your car. If you have no insurance, you can have your driver's license suspended or revoked. None of this is likely to be a surprise; what might become a surprise is what happens if you get sued or agree to a settlement that results from an automobile accident, and you do not have insurance.

If you have teenagers starting to drive, you know your premiums are going to go up. Car rental agencies figured out the risk of young drivers a long time ago; you have to be 25 to sign a car rental agreement, which is a point to remember when you have to add another driver to your policy. Remember to check into the per-accident and per-person payout amounts as well. They make a difference.

Car insurance only pays out as much as the limits in your policy. If you want a cheap premium and do not bother to look at what those payouts are, you could end up having to pay a considerable sum. Getting your hands on hundreds of thousands of dollars is not easy for most people, so part of your estate planning is checking into your automobile coverage and deciding whether it is adequate.

Umbrella liability insurance

This kind of policy provides added protection for your property that goes beyond homeowner's, renter's, automobile, or any other kind of insurance. If the person you rear-end at a red light thinks you have a good amount of money, he might stop by the We-Will-Sue-For-You law firm with dollar signs in his eyes. It is not fair that you should have to defend yourself against a frivolous lawsuit, but better that than losing your house or other property because you did not have adequate protection.

When looking into this kind of insurance, it is important to know what is and is not covered. Look for loopholes that will allow the insurance company to wiggle out of paying a claim.

An umbrella policy is not going to be necessary for everyone, but it is often essential to estate planning for people with a high-value estate because they have plenty to lose before they have a chance to pass it on. An insurance agent who tells you anything to the contrary needs to be crossed off your list.

Shopping around for an insurance agent you can trust is going to take some time, but the benefits are valuable. Making sense of all the possible options and then understanding the fine print of all those options — not to mention the legalities of making changes and still having your beneficiaries receive what you expect them to receive — is only going to happen if you do your homework.

Details, Details

It is all about the details when it comes to any kind of insurance; so, be sure to ask plenty of questions, and be extremely clear about what can, might, should, and will not happen related to your policies. Ask the hard questions, and do not accept anything less than a full response:

- Under what circumstances will the benefit not be paid? Find out all degrees of risk, including the worst-case scenario.
- Which of my assets are at risk and from what?
- What kinds of safety nets can insurance provide?

- What kind of insurance does not have a good cost/benefit balance, considering the details of my estate?
- What amount of coverage is excessive for my situation?
- Are there varying degrees of risk among my possible choices? If so, what are they?
- Why would my estate-planning team reject your recommendation?

Policies

With so many options, selecting what you need can be difficult. Check off those you think you might like to include in your estate plan, and then work with an agent to determine whether you need this kind of coverage.

While you are alive:

— Medical

— Dental

— Vision

— Disability — long-term

— Disability — short-term

— Long-term care

— Homeowner's/renter's

— Car

— Umbrella liability

After death:

— Life

— Whole life

— Universal life

— Joint first-to-die or second-to-die

— Term life insurance

— Annual renewable

— Decreasing

— Level

— Group

— Funeral/burial

Insurance for After You Are Gone

Some insurance agents will tell you that all you need is plenty of life insurance to make sure your loved ones are taken care of. Nod politely and then suddenly recall your breakfast/lunch/dinner with Uncle Greg that you completely forgot about. Leave immediately.

Insurance is not that simple. As with wills and trusts, there are many variations on this protection theme. The following are different types of life insurance:

- **Whole life:** Sometimes called cash value life insurance, this is the kind of policy most people know: After being qualified — smoker/nonsmoker, desk jockey/bungee jumper, age 25/age 75 — the insured person pays a monthly premium on a policy that will, upon his or her death, pay a predetermined, fixed amount of money to his or her beneficiaries. A portion of the fixed (it will never go up or down) premium is invested, and another portion is placed into an account, such as a savings account, and that cash value is accessible to the policy owner. It can be borrowed against as a loan, or the cash can be taken as the proceeds of the policy instead of the death benefit payout.
    - **Universal life:** A kind of whole life policy that guarantees a minimum return, but the value of the policy can go up or down. If the policy makes more money, the return might be high enough to cover your premium payments.
    - **Joint first-to-die or second-to-die**: Just like it sounds, this is a policy held by two people, and the beneficiary is paid after the first person or second person dies. You decide the payout when you set the terms of the policy.
- **Term life insurance:** Carries an annual premium and pays a specified death benefit to the beneficiary, but it does not have a cash value, so you cannot borrow money from it. The only payment made is to the beneficiary. The premium is based on the amount of insurance you purchase — what will be paid out after your death — and how

old you are: Younger people pay less, and, as they get older, their premiums rise accordingly. If you stop paying premiums, the death benefit is not paid. There are a number of different kinds of term policies available:

- **Annual renewable:** A policy that has an annual premium and can be renewed from year to year. Be sure you understand the renewal rights before signing.
- **Decreasing:** Premiums remain the same, but the benefit decreases over time. For example, if you purchase this kind of insurance to pay off your debts after you die — also known as mortgage or credit term insurance — the mortgage you want to insure is $250,000 at the time you purchase the insurance, but the mortgage value when you die is $150,000; the policy pays $150,000. This kind of insurance is recommended only for those who cannot get any other kind of insurance.
- **Level:** Coverage is guaranteed for a specific period of time, or term, such as five, ten, or 20 years at a specific premium. The premium will remain for the five-year period, but at year six, it will go up and remain at that rate through the tenth year, continuing in that direction.
- **Group:** Employers frequently purchase a term life policy for each employee as an added benefit. Employees get an exceptionally low rate, and there is no income tax on the premiums for the first $50,000 of coverage.

• *Did You Know?* •

In order to receive the death benefit from a life insurance policy, a death certificate for the policy holder is required as proof of death.

The most expedient way for your executor to obtain a copy is through the mortuary or other institution that is responsible for handling the body of the deceased. Copies can also be obtained from the county health department.

☑ Watch Out for This

- ☐ Authorized copies of a death certificate are needed to provide proof of death. As with a birth certificate, you cannot just reproduce a few dozen at your local copy center.
- ☐ Obtain several copies of the death certificate. Most institutions that require a certificate for proof will retain it for their files.
- ☐ Money will change hands, so call the county health department to find out the current fee.

Varying Beneficiaries

No matter what kind of insurance you decide to purchase, you can choose different beneficiaries depending on what the policy is going to do. To start, consider the goal of the policy, per the opening section of this chapter, and then who will need or use that money for that purpose. A life insurance policy that is specifically set up to give your family time to grieve might name your spouse as the beneficiary because he or she, not your estate, will pay the utility bills and buy the groceries.

No matter whom you name as the beneficiary, it is important to name an alternative beneficiary. If the first beneficiary dies before you or declines the gift, the second person or institution named will receive the benefit. If the death benefit goes unclaimed, then it is added to your estate and heads to probate for distribution by the court. Creditors and others may get more of the money than family, friends, or a charity you wish to support depending on what is owed at the time of your death.

There will be tax implications for all beneficiaries, some more significant than others. A life insurance policy payout is taxable income, so you might want to consider making your spouse or minor children the beneficiaries. They can take advantage of the marital and minor child exceptions, respectively, to avoid having to pay income tax. You could also make a life insurance policy payable to a charity; their tax-exempt status means they do not have to pay tax, and your estate gets to use the charitable deduction for estate tax purposes.

Another way to get around the income and estate tax implications is to transfer ownership of your policy to someone else. If your granddaughter holds your life insurance policy, then she owns it and names the beneficiaries, not you. The advantage of this setup is that your estate will not own the policy and have to pay taxes on the death benefit. That does not remove the income tax implication for the beneficiary, but it does reduce the amount of times that money can be taxed.

If your life insurance policy is already in place in your name and you want to make that transfer, be sure to consult with a tax specialist because that gift could be subject to state and federal gift taxes. Add on the income tax implication for someone who does not have an exemption, such as a spouse or a minor child, and it might not be such a good idea after all.

Then there is the three-year rule. If you transfer ownership on your life insurance policy and you die within three years, the death benefit is added to the value of your estate and is subject to state and federal estate taxation.

Case Study: Insurance: More than Life Coverage

Linda Horn

Chief Executive Officer

Capital Concepts

linda@capitalconcepts.net

www.capitalconcepts.net

Some people only buy insurance, and others diversify their investments.

What is the benefit of having a large amount of insurance?

Tax-free income to your family or a charity is a benefit. Proceeds from a policy are often used to provide additional funds to pay the estate taxes.

Should you own a business or farm, insurance becomes critical to paying federal and state estate tax, due within nine months of your death. Or perhaps you wish to leave a legacy for future generations or name a charity to continue your legacy.

What are the drawbacks of a large amount of insurance?

The premium payment should never create a financial hardship. After all, life is about living.

Under what circumstance might an insurance company not pay out a death benefit on various types of insurance? (e.g., whole life, term life, accidental death)

During the first two years from the issue date, the policy can be contested for suicides or false statements on the application about known medical history that can be attributed to your death. After two years, or if the above does not apply, all claims are paid.

How is disability insurance a valuable part of estate planning?

Disability is often overlooked, when in fact you have six times the probability of becoming disabled while on the job than of dying on the job. Your largest asset is your income. Protecting your income far exceeds your home, yet we would never consider having no homeowner's coverage.

What other types of insurance, beyond life, are important to an estate plan?

Long-term care insurance is an essential part of your plan. Should you need long-term care, such as in a nursing home or assisted living facility, your assets will quickly be diminished and little will be left for you spouse or children. Waiting until you know you need it is like insuring your home when it is on fire; you cannot get it, and if you could, it would be very expensive.

What are the benefits of working with an insurance professional?

If you are doing or have done your job of saving properly, a full-time professional is as necessary as the family doctor. A financial adviser works full time for many years to gain the expertise to get you to your final destination with as few bumps in the road as possible. Approximately 95 percent of do-it-your-selfers lose money, while the use of a professional is just the reverse. The discipline of a balanced approach to risk management and investment will pay off. A good adviser will make you far more money than you ever pay them. Their access to information alone is worth the investment. You do not drill your own teeth or cut your own hair, so why on earth would you invest your life savings with an amateur?

How does a person go about choosing an insurance professional? What characteristics or experience should a potential client look for?

First, ask trusted friends for their recommendations. Second, ask the adviser about their training, years of experience, education, and designations. What is their investment track record and philosophy? Do they share your values and understand you and your goals? Ask for a list of clients you can speak with. And last, go with your gut.

CHAPTER 8

Retirement Accounts

The "golden years" is public relations speak for that time in your life when your hair is white or gray, you do not have to set your alarm clock to get up in the morning, and you get to have some fun.

People who have access to some kind of pension plan or retirement fund can enjoy traveling or taking the grandkids out for ice cream and returning them all sugared-up to their parents before heading home. Some who might have done a little saving for retirement and reach the age of 65 — or 67, if you were born after 1960 — can consider their social security income as extra money, not essential for day-to-day living expenses. The group nobody wants to be in is the one that has little or nothing set aside for retirement, because the monthly payment from social security — $1,000 to $2,500 — almost certainly is not going to be enough to live on.

Every one of these scenarios, and a range of others you can imagine, all have implications for your estate planning. Most retirement planning sets a target for how much money you think you will need when you retire so that you can finally stop working. But that plan is an estimate, and things can happen that mean you have additional or less money than is needed. That means you will have added or fewer properties in your estate when you die.

The cost of living can be higher than you anticipated. Maybe you end up with the guardianship of your grandchildren at the age of 70. Or the trip to Mongolia was an absolute blast but ended with a broken leg when you fell off a camel, and you now have physical therapy bills piling up.

Your Nest Egg

The money you set aside for retirement is yours to keep or lose, depending on the kinds of investment strategies you follow. Looking at the retirement savings plans you have is part of the estate inventory you will find in Chapter 10, but some basic knowledge about what retirement resources people often have is a good place to begin. You might decide you need to make some changes or want to add a newly available method of saving.

You perhaps have some knowledge of your retirement plan — the human resources department at your company might have mandated a meeting every time a policy change was implemented. But what that means within the context of estate planning is different than the context of deciding how much money to take out of your paycheck every week.

Different companies offer different kinds of retirement plan options, and these have changed dramatically over time. Beyond the ever-shifting laws regarding what gets taxed and what does not, many companies have scaled back their participation in retirement plans. Once offered as a virtually guaranteed benefit, pension plans and contributions to retirement accounts are no longer reliable. Like any benefit, it is a perk, not mandatory or guaranteed by law, like being paid for the work you do.

It is important to know the kind of retirement program in which you participate and the obligations — if there are any — of the entity offering that plan. Professional associations and various government agencies also have retirement plans available, but their plans tend to be a little different. Once you know what type of plan you have, then you can see how that fits into your estate plan.

Employer pension plans

There are many variations on this theme, so this list will not be exhaustive. It is a place to learn a few things before you go chat with your estate-planning people. Pension and 401(k) plans are the most common ways employers provide a retirement benefit for their employees.

A pension plan is a program that is set up by an employer, including government agencies, to pay employees benefits upon retirement. Each employee has an individual account, and the employer contributes to each employee's account based on the terms of the plan.

There are two common types of pension plans. One is a defined benefit plan from which the employee will receive a specified amount of money upon retirement; the amount of the disbursement made is based on the number of years of employment. The second is a defined contribution plan, which sets a specific amount — a set percentage of income — the employee will put into the plan and makes payments only for the amount of money an employee has contributed to the plan.

A qualified pension plan means the amount of money that the employer puts into an employee's account is not taxed as income during the fiscal year the contribution is made. That means the income is tax-deferred — the taxes on that money are paid when it is received by the employee in the form of a monthly pension payment.

The following conditions exist:

- **Cost-of-living adjustment:** Some plans will have a variable that will allow for annual increases in the payments made to the employee to help cover the cost of rising prices. Not all plans have this feature.
- **Joint-with-survivor pension**: When an employee dies, her benefits will be paid to her spouse for the remainder of his life. If your spouse waives that right, then the employee's pension payments will

be larger — no need to set aside extra money for future payments — and the pension payments end when the employee dies.

- **Survivor benefit:** A portion of the deceased employee's pension paid to the surviving spouse. The amount, frequently a percentage, is set by the terms of the pension plan rules.
- **Waiver:** A written statement declining the right to receive benefits, signed by a spouse. This waiver must be signed to legally sever the right to claim any benefits. An alternative agreement, such as a prenuptial agreement, will not be enough.
- **Limits:** There can be some maximum annual payouts on some pension plans.

A company can avoid putting cash into a retirement fund, by distributing profits or shares of the company's stock. With a profit sharing plan, employees receive a portion of the profits earned by the company; the plan determines the amount that will be contributed to each employee's account. The funds can also be used to invest in programs for things such as a disability or medical plan.

Stock bonus plans are established by an employer to give shares of a company's stock to employees. When the employee receives the shares, he must pay taxes based on the value of the stock. An ESOP is a kind of stock bonus plan. The employer contributes shares of its stock to a qualified trust, and the employee only pays taxes based on distributions they receive.

Before an employee can receive any distributions or take full ownership of a pension plan, the employee has to be vested, meaning that they meet the predetermined requirements contained within the plan, based on the number of years they have worked for the employer.

Many employers set up a scale of ownership based on the number of years served. For example, if you only work for the company for two years, you are not vested at all, but when you reach three years, you become 15 percent vested. That means you can take ownership of 15 percent of the company's contribution to your pension plan, plus whatever funds you have contributed. Over time, the percentage of your ownership increases, and at any point beyond the 0 percent mark, you will be able to take your contributions and whatever vested percentage you have achieved.

More common today is the 401(k) plan. The equivalent of this plan for not-for-profit entities is the 403(b) plan. Named after the IRS code number defining this kind of plan, the 401(k) allows contributions to be made automatically by your employer via deductions from your paycheck. The advantage is that the money is taken out before taxes, so the amount you pay in taxes now is reduced. You will still have to pay taxes on that money and the interest it earns until you withdraw money from the account. The employer can make a matching tax-deferred contribution to your account. You can take the plan with you when you leave an employer, but the funds must be invested into another approved retirement plan within 60 days, or there will be taxes to pay. In addition, the percentage of the employer contribution you can take with you will likely depend on the vesting schedule for that plan.

Before talking about how you get all this retirement money, there are a few other retirement options to look at.

IRAs and Then Some

A retirement plan option that some companies use can also be used by individuals. An annuity is an investment that you create by contributing a specific amount of money over a predetermined period, with a fixed rate of return for a number of years. The money you put into an annuity is not tax-deductible, or taken pretax from your paycheck, if it is an employer-sponsored plan. There will be a distribution made to the annuity beneficiary for a fixed term — a specific number of years. The distributions will begin at a predetermined date — typically, the year you retire, so that you will be in a lower income tax bracket — and the distributions will be subject to income tax. The interest on the annuity is accumulated tax-free but will be taxed upon distribution. Here is an example:

> In 2008, Rob purchases an annuity from an insurance company for $60,000. The terms of the agreement stipulate that Rob will fund the annuity with ten annual premium payments of $6,000. For ten years, starting in 2018, Rob will receive $9,000 a year from the annuity. The idea is that in 2018, Rob will retire and his tax bracket will be lower than when he was working full-time. Now he will pay lower taxes on that money.
>
> Those annual payments Rob will receive beginning in 2018 will include the income he earned from the annual premiums he paid, which accumulated tax-free while the annuity was being funded. The only taxable portion of each $9,000 annuity payment Rob gets will be $3,000, because $6,000 of that came from the premium payments he made to fund the annuity. So, for a $60,000 investment, the final value of the annuity will be $90,000.

The return on this investment is low, so it appeals to people who do not feel comfortable with a high-risk investment strategy. A variable annuity is based on the same concept, but the funds are invested in the stock market, so the return depends on how well or poorly the economy does.

If you are self-employed, there is a retirement savings plan with a funky name for you as well. The Keogh plan — pronounced "key-oh" — is a qualified retirement plan for sole proprietors and partners, but your employees can also use it. The restrictions, distributions, and other details are similar to a defined contribution plan or defined benefit plan.

An individual retirement account (IRA) is just what it sounds like: a retirement account you set up for yourself. There is a limit to the contributions you can make annually. There is a tax deduction for making these contributions every year, so technically they are tax-free contributions. The taxes come after you withdraw the money, at a time when you are in all probability earning less money, so the amount you pay will be lower — which is one of the main selling points for this kind of retirement investment. You can hold onto these funds until the age of 70 and a half, but after that, the payments will begin.

The next generation of the IRA is called the Roth IRA. Named after its primary legislative sponsor, Senator William Roth from Delaware, contributions to this IRA are not tax deductible in the year they are made, however the interest earned while the money is invested will be tax free if you own the Roth IRA for at least five years. There are limitations on how you can invest the money in your Roth account, and there are big penalties if you take the money out before five and a half years have elapsed, but you can begin distributions that early if you meet the conditions. This IRA also has a distribution requirement that kicks in at age 70 and a half.

Your Government Nest Egg

Social security, Medicare, Medicaid: Most people have heard the terms and been told this is a safety net for those who have absolutely no other resources on which to rely when they are no longer able to work or are legally entitled to receive government benefits. That regular Federal Insurance Contributions Act (FICA) deduction, painfully visible on every paystub you ever received, is what makes up these government benefits.

The Social Security Administration now sends out annual reports breaking down your contributions and an estimated payment that you are likely to receive. If you are not getting one, you can go to **www.ssa.gov** and find out what is going on. Even if you have not yet seen one of those statements, it is a safe assumption that it will not be enough to pay all your bills when you retire. It is still important to have some understanding of how much of your money the government will give back to you, how it will affect your taxes, and also the taxes your beneficiaries will pay (yes, social security benefits are taxable income).

Social security retirement benefits

The retirement income provided by social security, commonly referred to as an old age benefit, depends on how many years you worked full time and paid into the system. If you meet the minimums — ten years of employment or 40 quarter-years — then you are considered to be fully insured. Those who have less than the minimum time in — younger people or those who have worked on and off over a long period of time — are called currently insured and are entitled to disability benefits only.

You can begin receiving old-age payments at the age of 65 — or 67, if you were born after 1960. If you decide to work while receiving benefits, the amount you receive can be reduced. There is an earning limit for various age ranges. But if you defer receiving your old-age benefit until later in your life, say age 69 or 70, your payments will increase.

Your social security payments do not have to be paid directly to you. You can designate a beneficiary for the full benefit or split it between you and another person. One-half of your payment can go to your current spouse, or you can designate an ex-spouse to whom you were married for at least ten years who has not remarried. Children can also receive half the payment while you are alive or 75 percent of the payment after you die; adopted children qualify, and under some circumstances, a stepchild might qualify. Grandchildren and widows or widowers can also receive benefits as long as they meet specific criteria.

Part of this old-age benefit is a lump-sum payment to the surviving spouse or child of the deceased to help with funeral expenses.

Social security disability benefit

If you are unable to work and you qualify as disabled — there is a list of disabilities that, according to the government definition of the word, qualifies or disqualifies you — then you can receive social security disability payments until you reach the age of 65. At that point, you begin to receive the social security retirement benefit at the same rate. The amount of money you receive depends on your work history, so there is no hard and fast number for this benefit. You can find more information at **www.ssa.gov/disability**.

Social security supplemental security income (SSI)

This benefit is for people who have very little (if any) property, or are blind or disabled in some other way. This is an absolute last-resort situation; it is good to know it is there if you need it, but doing everything possible to avoid that need is an excellent idea.

Medicare and medicaid

These terms are not interchangeable, even though they both are a medical benefit. Medicare is a medical insurance program offered by the federal government to people who are 65 or older, certain disabled people under the age of 65, and anyone with permanent kidney failure. This last one was added in 1972 out of a concern that people needing life-sustaining dialysis might not be able to afford it. Part A of this coverage is hospital insurance, and Part B is medical insurance. Part B now comes with a monthly premium.

Medicaid is a state-run medical plan that is supported by federal funding and provides minimal medical benefits for the financially needy. To qualify for this plan, you can only possess a set dollar amount in property — $2,000 is a common limit, but different states set different caps for single and married people. Michigan has a general asset cap of $3,000, but what constitutes countable assets and income for Medicaid eligibility in Michigan is complex. It is best to sort out specific situations with the Michigan Department of Community Health. Because medical bills can be extremely high, it is entirely possible that a serious illness could devastate your savings and make it necessary to take advantage of this program, so it is important to be aware that it is available if needed.

Protecting Your Eggs

Estate planning is about protecting your property, and that includes the nest eggs and the baskets that hold them. In addition to estimating what money you will be spending from your retirement accounts, you need to consider what might or might not be left in those accounts after you die. You need to do some additional research to make sure what you expect will be there.

Is your pension plan insured?

The Pension Benefit Guarantee Corporation (PBGC) is a federal agency that can insure and therefore protect some or all of your pension, if your plan qualifies for the coverage and your company purchases the insurance. Not all pensions are insured, and if they are, it might only be for a percentage of each account. You should contact your employer's human resources office to find out more information on whether your pension is insured.

Lump sum payments

Be wary of any retirement investment that offers a lump-sum payment over annual distributions. This kind of plan assumes the company will be in business and have the necessary funds when you retire. However, given the way formerly indestructible investment institutions and financial companies are falling, there is no guarantee.

Company stock contributions

If your company matches your retirement investments with their own stock, it is a good idea to diversify your holdings as much as possible. If selling your company stock is an option, most likely after you are fully vested, then consider doing that. Company loyalty is one thing; risking your financial security on any one company is a dangerous investment strategy — think WorldCom, Enron, and Bear Stearns. It is not about your commitment to your employer, but your responsibility for your own future.

Medicare supplemental insurance

Medicare is a wonderful benefit, but it is not perfect. There could be times when Medicare will not pay for some treatments, medications, or doctors you need. If you have health issues, it might be a good idea to investigate and invest in Medigap insurance, an insurance plan specifically designed to pay for Medicare exclusions.

Beneficiaries and their taxes

Always name beneficiaries for any retirement resources you have. If you do not name a beneficiary and a substitute, then the money in those accounts will be added to your probate estate and be subject to the claims of creditors and taxation by state and federal governments. Also, make sure that your beneficiaries know they have been named and what the tax implications might be if they receive those funds. You might decide to make sure your estate provides them with enough money to cover the taxes. *This was discussed further in Chapter 4.*

Retirement/Estate Planning Strategy

Now that you have an idea of the breadth and scope of retirement savings plans and the resources available to you through the U.S. government, you need to decide how you want to use or save that retirement money.

You can decide to spend it all. You might want to completely exhaust all your retirement funds — after all, that might be why you saved all that money. That way, you do not have to worry about paying the bills when you want to stick your toes in the sand. Your remaining property is your backup plan. Whatever is left when you die is what you leave to others.

Then there is the frugal approach — choosing to link your retirement needs and spending with your estate planning so that you estimate what you will need until you die, and then add a cushion to preserve the bulk of your estate for your spouse, children, grandchildren, and others.

By using this last approach, you take into account tax payments and future security for the people and organizations that mean the most to you. This is much more work and adds other considerations, such as inflation and keeping up with tax laws. But it is your money, and if you want to have a say in what happens to it when you no longer have a voice, then this is the best way to do that.

Case Study: Retirement Accounts and Estate Planning

Howard McEwen, CFA

Makris Financial Group, Inc

How much of an impact does a retirement account make on an overall estate plan?

It is important to remember that a will does not dictate the beneficiary of retirement plans, such as 401(k)s and IRAs.

The owner of each of those types of plans is allowed to designate a beneficiary. How the beneficiaries are treated is laid down by the 401(k) or IRA's custodial agreement. This custodial agreement overrides anything a will has to say.

Owners should do and look for the following:

- Make sure they designate a primary beneficiary — who gets the money when you die.
- Make sure they designate a contingent beneficiary — who gets the money if you die and your primary beneficiary is dead.
- Make sure that the custodial agreement allows a per stirpes designation. "Per stirpes" means that if one beneficiary dies, that beneficiary's heirs will be entitled to those assets.

- If needed, make sure beneficiary restrictions can be put in place. If someone is young or has special needs, getting a large chunk of money at your death might not be the best thing for them.
- Regularly review beneficiaries, make sure you have records of who they are, and let your heirs know where those records can be found.

Any negative impact on estate planning is not tremendous if the retirement accounts are managed properly. The primary thing is to keep beneficiary designations up to date.

For example, take my client Johnny Jones, who came to my office several years ago. Johnny is a widower in his late 70s. He had a daughter and two sons. His daughter, Irene, was married with two children. His eldest son, Max, was married with three children. Bob, the baby of the family, never married and had no children. Bob also had some brushes with the law and is still wrestling with addiction problems.

Johnny retired from a large Fortune 500 company after 30 plus years of work. His main asset was his 401(k) plan that he rolled over into an IRA when he retired. Johnny did not consider designating a beneficiary. In fact, he did not remember discussing it with his adviser.

After growing dissatisfied with his old adviser, Johnny came to my firm. Unfortunately, his eldest son, Max, had died in an industrial accident three years previously. I noticed on his current statements that Max was still listed as a beneficiary.

"Yeah, I just hadn't gotten to that yet," said Johnny.

After looking over the custodial agreement, I explained what would happen to Johnny's money if he happened to die without updating it.

"The custodial agreement does not provide a per stirpes provision," I told him. "What this means is that if you die right now, only Irene and Bob will get any money. Max's kids will be totally disinherited."

"You mean, even though he is still on there, his share will not pass on to his kids?"

"Right," I said. "If Irene and Bob decided to disclaim a portion (basically say, 'I do not want Dad's IRA'), Max's kids might inherit — if the courts decide that way. But there are no guarantees that Irene and Bob or the courts will carry out your wishes in this case."

"Also, how will inheriting a large sum of money affect Bob? He is already dealing with addiction issues. Could getting this inheritance actually kill him?"

These are blunt questions with a simple answer: keep an updated beneficiary designation form, designate those beneficiaries per stirpes, and restrict what kind of money Bob would inherit.

Is there anything a person can do to maximize their retirement plans?

I consider two ways to maximize a client's retirement plan. First is predeath, by properly allocating a client's account with regard to their risk-reward profile. The second is post-death.

Here is how: In the custodial agreement of the IRA or 401(k), they should verify that their beneficiaries could perform a stretch IRA.

For the majority of Americans, an IRA or 401(k) is their largest asset. By stretching that IRA across multiple generations, an IRA owner can create tremendous wealth for future generations of his family.

How do you stretch an IRA? Simple: by withdrawing the absolute minimum necessary to meet IRS regulations. The funds that remain in the IRA are allowed to compound tax-deferred over a number of years.

Here's a simple example:

David Johansen is married to Patty. They have one son, Sami. Sami has a daughter — Chrissie, age one, the apple of her grandparents' eye.

Sami is financially self-sufficient, so David designates Chrissie as the sole primary beneficiary on one of his IRAs that Patty will not need if he should die.

In the year David turned 70 and a half, the IRS mandates that he withdraw a percentage of his IRA. This is so they can take it. In that first year, the withdrawal is 3.65 percent.

David takes this withdrawal and then dies.

Chrissie becomes the owner of that IRA, now worth $100,000. Because it was her grandfather's IRA, she is still required to make withdrawals, but those withdrawals are based on her age — not her grandfather's.

Thus, that first year, one-year-old Chrissie would have to withdraw $1,225. The IRS tables provide a life expectancy of 81.6 years for Chrissie, so $100,000 / 81.6 years = $1,225. If the IRA earns an average of 8 percent over Chrissie's life expectancy, her grandfather's IRA would have paid her $8,167,629.

Scenic sunset in the dunes of Northern Michigan

Historic Tower in University of Michigan Campus, Ann Arbor

CHAPTER 9

Setting Priorities

Estate planning is more than just deciding what to do with your stuff after your death. Some thought needs to go into what you want to do and how you want to try to prepare for the things you can and cannot predict. A crystal ball to look into the future is wishful thinking, but an even better resource is close at hand — the past. By making time to review the decisions and choices you have already made in your life, you will be able to see what has been important to you.

When you had an opportunity to invest in your 401(k) at work, did you put in the maximum amount allowable, a modest percentage of your income, or defer investing until later? Are you glad you made the choice you did, or would you do things differently based on what you know now?

The answers you come up with are an example of how to begin making some decisions. By looking at what you used to think about financial matters, the change in the mix of people in your life, and the organizations you used to support in order to compare that against your present situation, you will be able to see patterns or inconsistencies that are important to the priorities you set for your estate.

This review also needs to include your current financial situation. The credit card debt you do or do not have is influenced by your view of the use of credit. If you do not have any credit cards, that says something about your views on the use of plastic for making purchases and whether paying interest on a purchase is acceptable. Maybe you have a small balance because in the same month you had replaced the tires on your car, the bottom of the water heater decided to drop out, and you simply did not have the cash to pay for a new one. Paying off that balance right away or letting it ride for a bit until you get back from your next business trip also says something.

It can be fun to reminisce about the unexpected adventure to South America with a college course you only took because of that cute guy or girl you thought you wanted to date. It can also be difficult, even painful, to remember a family beach vacation that ended up with Grandpa in the hospital and dying three months later. But if you make the effort, you might be able to recall how much fun he had preparing for and involving you and the other kids in the crab boil at sunset, and that will inspire a desire to share that experience with your grandchildren.

The essential part of this process is being attentive to the insignificant, the significant, and everything in between. All these things can serve as helpful pointers now and potential visions for the future.

Your Own Who's Who

Even though every person in your life might not end up in your will, considering the people who are important to you, and those who are not, is one way to identify what matters most to you. Because you are considering your priorities for yourself in addition to your family, friends, and maybe even professional associates, a review of people connected to those priorities makes sense.

The most obvious important people are your family and closest friends. Most people can rattle off the names of people they are related to by birth, marriage, or mutual agreement — friends frequently become "chosen family." A bit more thought might be needed when considering extended family or distant relatives.

It might be a given that family is so important to you that everyone living in your house will sit down to eat at least one meal together every day, often dinner; kids home from college or the grandparents visiting from out of state for a week all know this is expected. It might also be known by your children that there are some family members they never see but for whom everyone signs the family holiday card each year; if those same people send a note with a small gift for a birthday or graduation, a thank-you note will be written, because those distant relatives are equally important. These relatives are always invited to parties even though they never come.

Priorities revealed:

- Time with family is more than important; it is essential.
- Every celebration that calls for a party begins with a call to family members to find out what dates work for them.
- Even though some relatives live far away or might even be reclusive, you make sure your children keep in touch; you want them to have a strong sense of family regardless of proximity.

Implications for estate planning:

- Immediate family is so important that you want to make sure they have what they need.
- A desire to leave something to every family member, be it cash or a memento
- Is everyone clear about how important your family is to you? Just because family time and ties are important to you does not mean your siblings, children, or anyone else will be aware of this. Clearly communicating this priority to your family is a good idea so that when the will is read and the distant relatives are included, the immediate family does not contest your bequests and your wishes are carried out.

People come and go from our lives at various times for different reasons. The people with whom you surround yourself now are probably a quite different mix when you consider the people from your past. Even though life circumstances play a part in that coming and going of people, the effort you make to include, or exclude, people from your life places a value on that relationship. If you go out of your way to call someone or delete a message from the answering machine with no intention of calling the person back, it says something about how you feel about that individual.

Looking at the changes in your personal circle is one way to approach this review of people. For example: After being widowed, you might have lost touch with your in-laws; this does not bother you because they never liked you or the fact that you married their son or daughter. The kids are old enough to go visit their grandparents when they want to.

You remarried and have become close to the extended family of your current husband or wife. This new, blended family includes an alcoholic uncle you simply cannot stand to be around, even though everyone thinks he is the life of every party. Similarly, when your kids get married, they do not want to have to juggle multiple Thanksgiving dinners because they embrace the blended family as positive and open. So, they propose a huge family gathering of all sides that results in meeting new family members with whom you now enjoy weekend camping trips and a weekly bowling league.

Priorities revealed:

- You want to have people in your life with whom you can have a friendly, healthy relationship.
- You are willing to meet familial obligations, such as making an effort with your in-laws when your wife was alive, but once an obligation is fulfilled, you are all right with letting it go.
- Distancing yourself from people who can be harmful to you or your family is also all right, but you try to do it in a manner that does not upset others.

- Family is important but not exclusive; "biological family only" events rarely happen because they feel exclusionary.

Implications for estate planning:

- Including people who are not related by blood in your will must be handled legally and carefully to avoid any contest after you are gone. State laws governing family inheritance are clear; the same cannot be said for non-relatives.
- Leaving money to a family member with an addiction or some other life problem — maybe an abusive spouse or unscrupulous children — might require the use of a trust and a trustee to avoid the potential disasters that can result.
- Consider not including someone in your will. Giving a significant bequest to a specific person might not sit well with you, but a small gift could be considered to avoid a contest due to complete exclusion.

The faces of people you call friends can also change over time. For example: Debbie, a friend from grade school with whom you kept in touch via letters when you lived in different states, is now a neighbor, thanks to her job transfer. The college roommate with whom you shared many late-night study sessions and much burnt microwave popcorn moved from experimenting with drugs to hard-core use. The last time he called you to bail him out of jail, you told him it was the last time, and you have not heard from him since.

Then there are the people we encounter just doing our everyday business. We can easily take them for granted, not realizing their importance until something happens. For example, there is Betty, the elderly woman who lives down the street and has no family. She ends up in a nursing home after breaking her hip, ending your Friday morning tea and cookies visits. There is the librarian who knows you by name and suggests books you might like. And there is the mechanic who normally changes the oil in your car, but one day is not there when you stop in. His son is at the register and explains that he was feeling tired and needed a few days off.

Priorities revealed:

- Your awareness of and concern for others extends beyond your immediate circle to acquaintances.
- Frequenting local shops and businesses is important to you; you go out of your way to avoid impersonal, big-box stores.
- You prefer to be a part of the community in which you live.
- Neighbors matter.

Implications for estate planning:

- Continuing to support the organizations and institutions you appreciate and which have been a source of friendships for you, such as your local library, when you are no longer around to cast your vote for a levy or make a donation might be added to your list of bequests.
- The support you give to a family-owned business might not be significant, but something in your estate might be helpful to them: Your mechanic might appreciate the tools you use for fixing your car.
- Donating your book collection to the local library would make your family happy; they are not big readers, and it would be one less thing to handle when it comes time to sell the house.

By taking time to consider people, you will naturally think of memories and specific milestones in life that are related. The things you experience directly or simply witness also provide an opportunity to review your priorities.

Memory Lane

Looking back to the mundane as well as the amazing through the filter of estate planning makes it possible to see how the past can inform and even direct the future. If you see accumulated knowledge and financial resources as the means to adding some adventure and comfort to the later years in your life, not just gifts for others, then you can live unfulfilled dreams or expand on some wonderful experiences.

Consider that trip to South America: Would you have begged, borrowed, or gone into debt to have the extra month in the rainforest, knowing you might never have the chance to go back? Look at this year's vacation plan. Are you going anywhere near a rainforest? Would you consider changing your plans to return to that place south of the border? Are you disappointed that you cannot change your plans? Would you like to go again if you could come up with the money for the trip? Or has the idea of some tropical disease soured you on that kind of adventure? Does a cruise ship that anchors off the coast and includes a one-day trip to the very edges of the greenery sound more like your idea of fun?

There are any number of events from the past that underscore the priorities you had at that time and how far you have drifted into another view of what is important. Here are a few memory joggers to get you thinking:

Family time:

- Vacations with immediate family only/large, extended gatherings.
- Annual visit from the cousins were fun/torture.
- Having a sleepover at a friend's house made you want to stay there/go home.
- Thanksgiving dinner did/did not include a "kids' table."
- How many parties were held at your house, and which ones did you enjoy or loathe?

School:

- Favorite subject/class
- Memorable teacher — the one that got you excited about learning and how he or she did that
- The class bully and how you handled him or her when it was your turn to be picked on
- Public or private? Liked or disliked? Why?

- Science fairs — participation by choice or force and the level of desire to hide under your display table during judging
- Fraternity/sorority/independent thinker?
- Class office positions held by election or appointment

Extracurricular:

- Scouting or made fun of scouts?
- Reporter for the school paper
- Band
- Helped teachers clean after school
- Clubs
- Sports

Do-overs:

- Your first/second/third marriage
- Rehabbing the cute bungalow that ended up selling for less than you paid
- Studying economics and only taking one art class in college
- Giving up your film cameras for digital
- Donating your turntable and all your jazz record albums
- Not touring Europe before having kids

These life experiences are more than just a reflection of how you used to feel or what you were forced into doing by your parents. Your recollections and the way you respond to them now are a measure of what matters to you now.

Maybe that beach house you rented in 1998 is exactly the kind of home you wanted to have when you dreamed of living in a beach house. Perhaps that dream is never going to come true, given the circumstances of your life, but there is still time to make changes right now. You have eight more years until you are fully vested in your pension fund, so you have eight years to plan. Prepare to sell your existing home in the suburbs; help your kids deal with the shock of your move to Nags Head, North Carolina, and get your finances in order. Your accountant and lawyer can get to work on the papers for the living trust you need to make sure your retirement years will be non-stop beach time.

If having fun in your life was something you passed up to fulfill obligations or deferred to achieve other goals, then you might decide recreation is so critical that you want to share that lesson with your grandkids. One way to do that is to make sure they have the "mad money" necessary to fund the fun; set up a "mad money" trust for each grandchild to do whatever they want in the summer between high school and college. Once you make that a priority — because their parents have already funded their tuition and other fees — you can figure out how much you need to save or how much you need to not spend from your retirement account to fund those trusts.

Reminiscing often includes groups of people with like-minded views and dreams. Those groups also matter when it comes to estate planning.

Your "People"

Not everyone has an entourage of groupies, support staff, and employees to do their bidding. More often, you are the one doing the work, and frequently it is for a nonprofit organization. Your priorities about which causes or institutions to support have most likely changed over the years. The arts, once a luxury on a limited budget, are now at the top of your annual giving list, but the Peace Center that was struggling to survive in the basement of the dilapidated building next to your first apartment has moved to the storefront and still gets 20 hours of your time every month.

The institutions that rely on your time, money, or donations of office supplies have captured your imagination or hopes, or maybe just inspired you with their underdog determination. Whatever the reason, they are important to you. While they consider you among their supporters, i.e., their people, the fact is that your desire to see them succeed makes them your people.

Considering the nonprofits you have supported at different times in your life might spark an interest to get involved or lend support again. Life changes, such as a parent dying of cancer, might inspire you to add the American Cancer Society or a hospice to the list of charities you wish to support.

Because estate planning is more than distributing belongings after you die, the importance you place on these groups needs to be factored into your priorities. Maybe the Peace Center is on the verge of needing to move because they are growing so rapidly. Or perhaps that old bakery building you bought a few years ago has not turned out to be the successful investment property your realtor swore it would be; putting it into a charitable trust or making an outright donation of it to the Peace Center might be the best way to help them and reduce the amount of real property in your estate.

If you do move to that beach house in Nags Head, the time you spend at the cat rescue shelter is no longer going to be an option. You know they desperately need volunteers, but even more desperate is a need for cat food. A donation of cash for the purchase of food is only going to be possible if you decide you want to do that and set up a way to make it happen.

After you fund the mad money trusts, make sure you have enough to live on during retirement and cover the cost of your disability insurance as the safety net; it might be that you only have enough in your estate to support two charities. Which will they be — the arts organizations, the Peace Center, or the cat shelter? Do you want to set aside a little extra in case you find some institution in Nags Head that you might want to support later?

These are the difficult decisions that must be made if you prefer not to work extra hours or cut into your current spending to allow for future expenditures.

Must-Do

The things you never thought you would get to do in this lifetime or the envious moments spent listening to others describe what you have always dreamed about doing inspires some people to create a "must-do" list. Be it mountain climbing or scuba diving, going out to dinner at a five-star restaurant, or taking two weeks off work to just stay at home and relax, the things you feel are important enough to put on a list are important enough to make happen.

Setting priorities for your estate planning is a means to that "must-do" end. Identifying what matters most right now and what you thought was important but now realize is no big thing makes it possible to consider financial decisions that will have an impact now and later.

Case Study: A Finance Coach for Estate Planning

Sue Holm, founder
Make Peace with Money
sue@makepeacewithmoney.com
www.makepeacewithmoney.com

CLASSIFIED CASE STUDIES™ directly from the experts

How should a person make decisions about their priorities?

All major decisions about financial priorities should be made with a trusted adviser or counselor. For some folks, that can be family or friends. For some, that is a financial planner or adviser. If someone has emotional issues about money, a financial counselor or coach or a therapist who is comfortable with money issues should be consulted.

There is an element of spirituality that also touches these decisions during life and when contemplating death. How much to give away? To whom? Why? When? Charitable giving, tithing (donating a fixed percent age of income to a religious institution), and giving back are all rich issues for discussion — among families, faith communities, and in our world.

Does charity begin at home? What does that mean? What does that look like? Is money good, bad, or neutral? Are money and spirituality linked or not?

How do people apply those priorities to their decisions about disbursing their money and property after their death?

By not planning, people allow the state to dictate the disposition of their money and property. For those who have priorities, familial or spiritual, those priorities will drive the nature of the disbursal.

Why do people fight over things like a toaster or a chair after someone has died?

Because they have unresolved emotional issues, either about themselves and their self-worth or their relationship with the deceased.

How can the person who owns the toaster or chair prepare his family for that situation?

If people are clear about their intentions in creating estate plans and have the occasion to discuss their intent with their family, it can defuse some of the tension. The person who owns things can create an atmosphere in which it is okay to ask for what you want while they are still alive. They can ask their loved ones what they need or want as a remembrance. They can create a system to disbursing things not otherwise specified in the will.

How often should those priorities be revisited?

Financial priorities should be revisited at all major life milestones — marriage, divorce, birth of children, the children achieving their majority (turning 18), birth of grandchildren.

What are the benefits of working with a financial counselor or coach?

The benefits include financial clarity, mastery, and ultimately peace with money. This manifests in decreased debt, increased saving, and earning what you are worth.

Many people do not know that financial counseling or coaching is available. Many people with financial issues know they need help; they just do not know how to find it.

A lot of people think that because they are smart and successful in most areas of their life, they should know what to do with money, or that they will be able to figure it out themselves. This can be increasingly frightening and frustrating as they try and fail on their own.

Among the most productive discussions between a financial counselor and client are those that involve the differentiation between needs and wants and how to prioritize them.

How should a financial professional collaborate with other people in an estate-planning team?

Ideally, during the financial counseling process, the counselor will refer the client to an estate-planning professional if the client does not yet have an estate plan.

Financial counselors can be an excellent resource for estate-planning professionals working with surviving spouses or partners who need or want some structure and support while they assume financial responsibility for themselves or for the estate.

Estate-planning professionals should consider referring clients who inherit sums of money or assets they are inexperienced in managing to a financial counselor.

How does a person go about choosing a financial professional? What characteristics/experience should a client look for?

As this is not a licensed or regulated field, it is important that clients examine the credentials of anyone they are considering as a financial counselor or coach. Training agencies, such as the Financial Recovery Institute (**www.financialrecovery.com**), frequently list those counselors or coaches who have been trained and certified.

Many clients seeking financial counseling have not talked about their money issues with anyone. They frequently have conscious and subconscious money secrets. It is imperative that clients trust their financial counselor, and that a financial counselor or coach be able to deal with the client's emotional issues that underlie the money issues.

Upper Tahquamen Falls, Michigan

CHAPTER 10

Choosing Who, What, How, When, and Why

Now that you know what you own or need to save and have an idea of what you will need to keep for yourself as you go forward and a sense of the people and organizations you would like to support with your hard-earned assets, it is time to put all that information together into a comprehensive estate plan. The detailed overview of the choices you have for delivering assets provided in Chapters 5 through 8 is just that, an overview. The legal restrictions and limitations of different kinds of trusts, annuities, insurance policies, and other financial vehicles will help you identify potential resources that will meet your goals. Only professionals in estate planning are going to be able to make your estate plan meet your goals and be legally binding.

Beyond the difficult choices of who gets what, you also need to choose the CPAs, lawyers, financial advisers, insurance agents, and others who will be a part of your estate planning and management team. Many of these people receive commissions for the sale of different kinds of products. The trust that might be best for you could have a smaller commission than the trust with plenty of extras — a planner who is doing his or her job will suggest what is best for your needs, not his or her checking account. Even though a less expensive firm might be attractive while you are still building up your estate, consider the longevity of the firm; there is the distinct possibility that later you will have a larger estate if you get proper guidance.

Something with such a long-term impact as your estate planning deserves a high level of care, thoughtfulness, and attention.

Who and When: The Matching Game

The solitaire game Concentration, referred to as "the matching game" by many preschoolers, involves placing all the cards in a deck upside down on a table in a grid pattern. Each player turns over two cards; if they do not match, then they are flipped back over, and the next player takes a turn. The goal is to keep flipping over cards and remembering where each one is so that you can make matches — two fours, two queens, two eights — until all matches are made, and the person with the most sets of matches wins. It is a good way to teach children how to increase their concentration skills, but the premise of the game is also a good method for distributing your estate. The key difference is that you decide what makes a match.

If you are unsure how to begin, consider the sticky-note method. Put the name of each person and institution you wish to support with your estate; include yourself in that list if you plan on creating a living trust or dedicating other resources to your retirement that will be a part of your estate plan. If the case of multiple beneficiaries — you benefit from a living trust during your life and there is a beneficiary for that trust after your death — be sure to note both people.

Make a sticky note for each asset that you listed on the Your Estate in Black and White Worksheet found in Appendix A of this book.

Now get the Prioritization Worksheet found in Appendix A of this book so you can compare what you think you want against the practical structure of the estate you are crafting.

Then lay them all out by matching them up, and see whether the matches are what you want them to be.

This method gives you the chance to see the differences in the amounts, property, and other bequests you make. That side-by-side comparison might also raise questions in your mind about the implications of the distribution.

> Carol tends to be a black-and-white kind of person, so she might get upset when she learns the difference in the value of the property she gets and the Nags Head property going to Danny — the property she gets is worth 50 percent less. The fact that her profession is rehabbing houses and that she can invest a small amount to make the property equal in value — if not more — is something you might want to explain. Or, you might decide to add some fixer-upper cash to her bequest to soften the blow.
>
> You might not feel right about giving Jeanine a $50,000 bequest when Mary Lynn is getting $60,000, even though you know it is what they need. Add a little something to Jeanine's bequest if that makes you feel better.

But then, all these differences might not bother you in the least. You know what you are doing and why, and because it is your estate plan, the issue of fairness is a moot point.

Another thing this exercise can do is provide an opportunity to consider bundling or separating items in your estate as part of a bequest. If you are looking only at the dollar value of a gift, packaging together the sentimental items with stocks, bonds, or cash will give you a chance to customize a bequest to the person who receives it.

> Mary Lynn is not a reader, so the book collection would not mean as much to her as Jeanine, who is getting her degree in creative writing.
>
> The charitable trust for the Peace Center that includes the old bakery is an incredibly generous gift — the largest they have ever received. That being said, the actual expense of the upgrades needed to meet building codes will take a big chunk out of their operating budget. The extra $10,000 can be invested until they are ready to do the work, and it is a way to motivate other donors to kick in some support.

It is not necessary to use sticky notes for this exercise, but it is important to note that a light breeze could blow away your efforts. Imagine how an overly enthusiastic pet can scatter pieces of paper that do not stick. A large dry-erase board or chalkboard serves the same purpose. Regardless of the method, the ultimate goal is simple: match up your priorities with the people and gifts you wish to give.

Once you have settled on who is getting what, taking a digital photo of your makeshift plan could be helpful later when you decide you want to make changes. *See Chapter 12 for more information on this.* You will have a record of your notes and can use that to reconstruct and revisit this process, or maybe you will want to show it to a financial adviser. Converting this information to an electronic document is a possibility by using a table in a word-processing document or using a spreadsheet program.

An estate plan is something you will need to revisit and change regularly, so consider keeping your notes and other planning documents for a while, at least until you are sure you have all the information saved in some other format.

When: Today, Tomorrow, or Later?

An important strategy for estate planning that goes unused by many is early gifting. The traditional or customary time for distributing an estate is after a person dies, but staying with the traditional can mean a larger estate and more taxes. A gift tax might still apply to the property you hand over early, but, given the rate of tax increase, it is entirely possible this could mean a lower tax bill for the beneficiary.

Another thing to consider is when the beneficiary will get the most benefit from the gift you make. Your estate is yours to dispose of how and when you choose; if you want to take advantage of an opportunity to help a relative or charity in need, and then you can factor that into your estate plan.

> Jeanine graduated from high school with an International Baccalaureate (IB) degree — a special education program offered by her

high school. She has changed her major from creative writing and is now majoring in political science in college. The whole family thinks she is making a bad decision and that she is too young to understand how she will be limiting her career choices to politics only. Why be a politician? Everyone knows women can only go so far before they hit a glass ceiling.

You see the potential Jeanine sees — and more. International corporations, government embassies, and a long list of opportunities await the person who has the background and understanding of multiple cultures and how to navigate the intricacies of governmental policy and social mores.

The cultural club she belongs to is planning a trip to Mongolia, and she desperately wants to go, but her education trust fund will not cover the expenses of the trip. She can legally go on the trip, but she does not have the cash. Because you want to encourage her passion and efforts to get a well-rounded education, not to mention some invaluable experience before graduation, you decide to create an education trust for Jeanine that specifically covers the cost of school-related travel.

Even though Jeanine will not receive any other money from your estate, you can remind yourself that she is getting an immediate benefit that will have long-term implications for her ability to build her own estate. It might be helpful to explain this to her, too.

Choosing to give some gifts early, putting conditions on other gifts, and the logic behind why you are doing these things all need careful consideration. If your family is competitive or has some other characteristics that could inspire resentment or other negative reactions — before or after your death — you might want to consider sharing your reasoning. This can be done in the form of a letter to each family member that will be opened after your death or at a one-on-one meeting in which you discuss the terms and conditions of your will and estate.

Regardless of how open or confidential you are about your financial matters, remember that, after you are gone, your ability to explain yourself is limited. When deciding the timing of your gifts, keep this in mind.

How: The Professionals

There is a host of people from which to choose your estate-planning team. Who does what and areas of specialty can get confusing. A CPA can address tax issues, but so can a lawyer who specializes in tax law. Which is better will depend on what your needs are. *Chapter 2 describes the important people making up your estate-planning team. Please refer back to that chapter for a review of the parties.*

The best way to determine who can help you with your estate planning is to look at your needs, preferences, and expectations. If the content of this book is the extent of your estate-planning knowledge, then you have much to learn before you can check "estate-planning documents prepared" off your to-do list. A professional with access to multiple resources of current information that is written for the consumer and who has the patience to answer questions will be essential for you. Someone who knows what a QTIP is without looking in the glossary might prefer to seek a professional who can provide more detailed information without getting overly technical.

Beyond that, the circumstances of your life and interests are going to impact the time you have to spend, your level of commitment to achieving whatever timetable you set for completion, and the people with whom you work. Traveling across town for meetings might not be possible if you are going to be caring for your 18-month-old twin nieces while your sister goes back to school for a semester.

Some things to consider before you begin putting together your estate-planning team are:

- **Interest level:** If a root canal without anesthesia sounds like more fun than estate planning, or you have a true desire to plan but lack the time to make it happen, then you have some sense of how much you do/do not want to engage in this process.

  Consider that 75 percent of the population does not do comprehensive estate planning before they die, but the U.S. and state governments have enough laws on the books to take control of and benefit from your lifetime of work and savings. Focus on the benefits of this hard work and consider the good things it can accomplish for you and those who matter most to you.

- **Deadlines:** Any significant milestones that are coming up sooner or later.

  If you have a three-month world tour planned for next year, it would be a good idea to get this wrapped up before you leave the country. If you are not going anywhere for the next few years, you can take this at a slower pace.

- **Health issues:** Even if you are healthy right now, your age and family medical history could impact your planning timetable.

  Grandma Nan lived to be 100, but all her sisters died of breast cancer in their 60s, and you are either age 24, 48, or 56. Your father-in-law died at the age of 40 of a massive heart attack, and your husband is 48 years old.

- **Family matters:** Collaborative relationships, disagreements, a marriage or birth, long-standing feuds, addiction struggles, helping with child care, and everything in between can impact your decision-making and the time you can commit to this process.

  The bickering between two siblings might inspire a desire to cut them both out of your will, while a newly married couple means one more person to add — maybe two, if baby makes three.

- **Charities:** Like families, organizations go through considerable change. Insignificant change, such as a staffing change, or significant change, such as building a new facility, could influence your time commitment to estate planning, in addition to your giving.

The Friends Meeting House where you study received the permits and approvals necessary to go forward with the construction of their new building ahead of schedule; instead of breaking ground in five years, they begin in eight months. You may need to revise when they receive the money you have left them.

Once you have made up your mind to follow through with this estate planning you have been avoiding, and you know what your schedule looks like — as much as anyone can — you need to consider the components and status of your belongings. If you are just beginning to build your estate, such a will requires fewer professionals than someone who has 32 years in the workforce and multiple resources to consider. Special circumstances can complicate the process for any estate of any value.

The following offers an example of the many factors that may come into play when developing your estate family.

Family:

Blended: his, his, hers, hers, and ours
Unconventional: same sex, interracial
Adoption: domestic or international
Foreign-born spouse: not a U.S citizen

Personal:

Career changes
Multiple relocations: domestic or overseas
Frequent layoffs
Mental health concerns
Felony arrest(s)

Income:

Structured settlements

Rental property
Inheritance
Royalties
Unemployment

Outgoing:

Child support
Alimony
Elder care for parents
Terminal illness

Whether these things affect you or your estate, they need to be taken into consideration. In addition to being information your estate planner will need to know — the firm you approach might not want to deal with estate issues related to people who are not U.S. citizens — they might have implications for your budget.

The adage, "You get what you pay for," is a good rule of thumb for the level of risk you take with your estate-planning team members if you make decisions based exclusively on the fees they charge. It is entirely possible that you will get lucky with phone-book roulette and stumble across a CPA who has your best interest at heart; and even though he has considerable experience, he is willing to charge next to nothing for his expertise because he wants you to keep your money. But the high-priced estate-planning firm, with more credentials than you have ever seen, is not necessarily going to give you the kind of service you need or collaborate with your other estate-planning partners.

The process of selecting the professionals with whom you will work requires some scrutiny of individual professional standards — credentials for a CPA, passing the bar exam (or not) — but some general expectations for this group of people can be defined. Consider the following when choosing a professional to assist you with your estate plan:

- Do you recognize the name of the school from which he graduated? What does he do to stay current with changes in financial markets?

- How many years of experience does this person have?
- What is the focus or areas of expertise for that experience and the duration in each area?
- Do they have a private practice, group practice, or corporate environment? Find out whether the expertise of others is readily available if a question or problem arises.
- Ask the Better Business Bureau and allied professional associations — the American Bar Association (ABA) for lawyers — for complaints, reprimands, or any other questionable business practices.
- Ask about the nature of relationships with the providers of the products the individual or firm offers; ask for a disclosure of commissions and other perks provided to the individual professional or firm.
- Review the website for current clients. Does the list include people with estates similar to yours, or are they "high worth" individuals and business owners? A firm that specializes in businesses might do personal estate planning as an aside for those companies, but that is not its area of expertise.
- Talk to previous and current clients or friends and associates who recommend, or are wary of, the person and/or company.

Once you have a short list of people to interview for your estate-planning team, prepare as much information as possible in advance of your first meeting. This will help you and the professionals you interview to quickly determine how they might, or might not, be able to help you craft your plan.

Case Study: Estate Planning Choices

Scott J. Malof, CPA/PFS
SS&G Financial Services, Inc.
Certified Public Accountants and Advisors
www.SSandG.com

What information should a person collect to prepare for this process?

When preparing for the estate-planning process, people should begin preparing a snapshot of where they are today. Create a family tree of personal details including ages and health status for immediate family members as well as those whom you might have to care for, such as an aging parent. Also remember guardian nominations for your minor children, trustee nominations that are part of a will or other estate options, executor nominations to execute your will, separation/divorce agreements, and tax returns for the past couple of years.

This snapshot should include all relevant financial information, including listings of assets and liabilities, details of all insurance policies, and current and future income streams. Your financial situation would include a detailed personal balance sheet listing all assets and liabilities, life insurance policy details, other insurance coverage such as disability coverage, and income and expenses now and in the future.

The last piece, and often the most difficult, is your goals and expectations including legacies.

What are the most overlooked loopholes or opportunities people miss when coordinating the financial aspect of their estate?

Here are a few:

- Not using up each spouse's applicable exclusion amount, both at the federal and state level. For example, you could leave everything to your spouse.

- Assuming the kids can divvy everything up fairly without fighting. This could be a mistake, not an opportunity.
- Not using a gifting plan.

How does the power of gifting affect an estate plan?

Currently, all individuals can give any other individual up to $13,000 annually without using up their lifetime applicable exclusion amount of $2,000,000. To the extent given away, this money is not included in the donor's estate at death.

Suppose a couple has two children, two surviving parents, and four grandchildren. This couple could give away $208,000 annually — eight people times $13,000 in gifts times two donors. If this were done for a period of 20 years, the donors could remove $4.16 million from their estate, excluding the impact of earnings over those years. This could have a taxable federal estate at the highest rate. Based on a 45 percent tax rate the saving would be $1,872,000.

The downside to gifting is relinquishing the control over the property. Also, giving large sums of money to minor children does not come without ramifications, both good and bad. This is why estate planning can be so hard for so many people. The answers are not always about saving the most money or passing down the most wealth. It truly comes back to meeting a person's wishes.

How do state laws and federal laws affect estate-planning choices?

Federal and state laws have an enormous impact on estate planning. When people are determining where they would like their property ultimately to go, they need to be cognizant of the legal ramifications of their choices. For example, the rules for the transfer of property in a community-property state vary from those in a common-law state. Knowledge of these rules will help people to plan accordingly.

Also, much of estate planning includes trying to minimize any transfer taxes that may come due. The amount of potential federal and/or state estate or gift tax has an enormous impact on the estate plan. For example, a couple with a $10 million estate could easily save over $1 million with some very simple estate-planning techniques.

If this couple implements a gifting plan over a number of years, the savings possibility goes up substantially. Currently, the highest federal estate tax rate is 45 percent, leading to quite a savings when the estate is properly managed.

Confidentiality is very important to many people — sometimes from the public, but also from other family members. State laws especially govern what information must be made public record through probate, or disclosed on a limited basis such as through trust reporting to beneficiaries. Clients need to determine how much they want the public or their heirs to know about what they have, how they are passing it, and to whom.

Escanaba Michigan Marina, Lake Michigan Dawn

CHAPTER 11

Planning Your Estate: Last Will and Testament in Michigan

As mentioned in our general discussion in this book, specific requirements for drafting valid wills are directed and controlled by the laws of each state. While there are some common principles, not all states are the same. It is always advisable to obtain legal counsel to assist you in drafting your last will and testament, especially if you have more than one residence in different states or if you draw up your will in a different state than where you live. You should consult an attorney to ensure your will conforms to the proper controlling state law, as it will likely differ in various states. Also, state laws change from time to time.

It is important to understand Michigan's statutory requirements for valid wills at the time you draft yours. Otherwise, your efforts to bequeath your property could fail; regardless of what you wrote down as your intent to distribute your property according to "your will," it will be the same as if you wrote nothing. You will have died intestate — without a will. In that event, your property will be distributed according to state law, possibly in ways you never imagined, and often at greater court costs.

According to current Michigan law, if you are a least age 18 and mentally competent to do so, you can make a will in the state of Michigan. Under the Michigan Probate Code, there are four types of wills that may be accepted for probate: (1) a simple standard will, individually prepared, signed, and witnessed; (2) a handwritten "holographic" will signed only by the testator; (3) a form will; and (4) an international will.

Simple Standard Will

A simple standard will is what everyone thinks of as a will. It is individually prepared in typed format, naming the various beneficiaries and wishes of the decedent. It must be signed by the testator and witnessed by at least two competent witnesses.

Holographic Will

Michigan is one of the states that recognize a holographic will, which is a document written either fully in the testator's hand, or, in Michigan, the important parts of it are written in the testator's hand, dated, and signed by the testator. The value of this type of document is that the testator (you) can sit down and write out the entire will without the need for witnesses and notaries. One of the simplest, shortest, and most famous of holographic wills was one that said, "All to wife."

The key to a holographic will is that the document must be fully and legibly written by hand, signed, and dated by the person who has died. It cannot be spoken on video or audiotape, or physically written by someone else on behalf of the testator. If it is written by someone else, it will be invalid unless properly signed or acknowledged by the testator and witnessed according to the requirements of other types of valid Michigan wills.

The holographic will must be written in the testator's hand, signed, and dated by the person making the will. Witnesses can still be used — and are recommended — but they are not a legal requirement for the holographic will to be valid. Anyone who wants to make a valid will in Michigan can write it out by hand in this way.

In other respects, the holographic will must still meet the basic requirements of all wills — that is, the person making the will must evidence that he or she is of sound mind, generally by saying so in specific wording, such as, "I am of sound mind and know what I possess and how I want to distribute it upon my death," or, "This is my last will and testament. I am of sound mind, and I freely state how my possessions shall be divided and dispersed upon my death." The point is to make clear that you know and understand who you are, what you own, and your own mind as to how you want to dispose of what you own when you die. A will written by someone who is mentally incompetent or under coercion or duress is not valid.

That you want your writing to be considered a will as opposed to a letter, memorandum, journal, reflection, list, or some other non-testamentary document is very important. If, after your death, someone challenges that your handwritten document is not your last will and testament, the court will be obliged to examine it to determine what you intended when you wrote it. Words like, "I declare this document to be my last will and testament" very clearly state that you intend the document to be considered your will. Michigan courts take the intent of the testator very seriously and consider such evidence.

There must be more than a "chance" that you may have intended your writing to be a will, though. An example in Michigan is the case of People v. Burton (1989). This was a murder case in which a document prepared by the defendant's wife was considered as to its admissibility as evidence and, in the course of the judicial examination, it was important to consider whether the document was the wife's holographic will. The prosecutor wanted the document admitted into evidence because statements in it implicated the defendant in committing the murder for which he was charged. Without belaboring the legal rule of hearsay, it is sufficient to say that the document could have been admitted as evidence against the defendant if it had passed the test of being a bona fide will. It did not. Here is why.

The document had some of those words that sound like a will. The court described it as follows:

"At issue is a less than 2 ¼-page handwritten statement, on 8 ½ x 11 inch paper, allegedly prepared by defendant's wife, Jearleane Burton. The statement is not signed nor dated. It begins as follows: "To Whom it May Concern: I, Jearleane Burton, being of sound mind [and] body, [and] soul, do [r]equest this letter to be valid, and my last will and testament." Immediately following is a two-page narrative explaining that Burton was in fear for her life and detailing the events surrounding the killing and mutilation of the victim by defendant. The writing concludes, "Anything I own that would [sic] please go to my mother and family."

The Michigan court refused to accept this as a legitimate last will and testament for several reasons. Although it was written in the wife's handwriting, acceptable under Michigan's holographic will law, it lacked other indicia of a true will: (1) it was not signed; (2) it was not dated; (3) the wife's intent appeared to be more related to incriminating her husband than to disposing of property, the latter being the fundamental central purpose for writing a will. Almost as an afterthought, she concludes with a "by the way" of leaving anything she owns to her parents. Simply stated, the controlling "intent" of the document was not for the disposition of property. The court explained as follows why such a document would not be accepted as a will.

"First, the only elements of the writing that are testamentary in nature are the first and last sentences of the 2 ¼-page document. The writing, as a whole, is not testamentary but more akin to a journal entry or confession. Second, no specific disposition of property is mentioned. The only dispositional sentence contained in the writing is obscure and, in context, reads like an afterthought. Had Mrs. Burton's narrative described a certain disposition or a particular property, its resulting reliability and authenticity may have brought it within the exception. The narrative, however, describes only the details of the crime with which defendant is charged."

The above case illustrates how a court might examine a person's intent underlying the writing of the document as well as the formalities required — e.g., date and signature. In the above example, the intent was found to incriminate the husband rather than distribute property upon death. If the testamentary intent to pass down property is found, then a detailed description of the property may not be required.

Holographic wills have been ruled to be legal when written on various types of substances. Ideally, the testator would choose a high rag content quality paper and ink that can reasonably withstand the rigor of time and then store the will in a safe place. Less traditional things have been used, such as shirts, wood planks, napkins, cardboard, paper scraps, and melon rinds. These will work if the controlling rules of testator's own handwriting, legibility, date, signature, soundness of mind, and intent to be a will are satisfied. It is said that Leo Tolstoy, the famous Russian writer, wrote out his last will and testament on a tree stump.

Nevertheless, unless decent pen and paper are not available in exigent circumstances, your last will and testament is not the place to express humor and eccentricity, not if your intent to make a valid and lasting will is serious and not if you do not wish your mental capacity in writing it to be questioned out of context. If a shirt, a plank, a napkin, etc., is all that is available and time is of the essence, of course that is a different situation — and you might say in the will, "This is all I have to write on."

Such exigent circumstances can be dramatically proved and are self-explanatory in some circumstances, where holographic wills have been honored. Many such examples have occurred in heartrending situations on battlefields where the documents amazingly survived the chaos and destruction of war, often on bits of paper and even on helmets. One well-known will was written in Saskatchewan, Canada in 1948. A farmer named Cecil George Harris, who had become trapped under his tractor wheel for 10 hours, carved his will into the tractor's fender with his pocketknife. It reads: "In case I die in this mess I leave all to the wife. Cecil Geo. Harris." Though rescued by neighbors eventually, Mr. Harris died two days later. The fender was removed from the tractor and filed with the court for probate. The court accepted it as his valid will. The fender and Mr. Harris' knife with which he carved his will are now on display in the law library at the University of Saskatchewan College of Law — after having resided for many years in the courthouse.

Not only were Mr. Harris' exigent circumstances self-explanatory, he had the incredible presence of mind to make it clear by referring to "this mess" in transcribing his simple will. Further, there were witnesses, not to the will itself, but to its circumstances.

Michigan Statutory Form Will

Another type of will permitted in Michigan is the completion of a fill-in form. This form is prescribed by statute. Michigan probate statute 700.2519 sets out the form as quoted below. Note the statutory will carries the warning that you must not cross out or add to any of the printed portions of the will, as doing so may invalidate it.

The form further directs that you have two, preferably three, witnesses attest your signature. The witnesses must not be anyone who receives a benefit from any bequest in the will.

MICHIGAN STATUTORY WILL OF ______________________________
(Print or type your full name)

ARTICLE 1. DECLARATIONS

This is my will and I revoke any prior wills and codicils.

I live in ______________________________ County, Michigan.

My spouse is ____.
(Insert spouse's name or write "none")

My children now living are:

________________________ ________________________

________________________ ________________________

________________________ ________________________

(Insert names or write "none")

ARTICLE 2. DISPOSITION OF MY ASSETS

2.1 CASH GIFTS TO PERSONS OR CHARITIES. (Optional)

I can leave no more than two (2) cash gifts. I make the following cash gifts to the persons or charities in the amount stated here. Any transfer tax due upon my death shall be paid from the balance of my estate and not from these gifts. Full name and address of person or charity to receive cash gift (name only 1 person or charity here):

____

(Insert name of person or charity)

____

(Insert address)

AMOUNT OF GIFT (In figures): $ ________________________

AMOUNT OF GIFT (In words): __________________ Dollars

____

(Your signature)

Full name and address of person or charity to receive cash gift (Name only 1 person or charity):

____

(Insert name of person or charity)

____

(Insert address)

AMOUNT OF GIFT (In figures): $ ____________________

AMOUNT OF GIFT (In words): ________________ Dollars

____

(Your signature)

2.2 PERSONAL AND HOUSEHOLD ITEMS.

I may leave a separate list or statement, either in my handwriting or signed by me at the end, regarding gifts of specific books, jewelry, clothing, automobiles, furniture, and other personal and household items.

I give my spouse all my books, jewelry, clothing, automobiles, furniture, and other personal and household items not included on such a separate list or statement. If I am not married at the time I sign this will or if my spouse dies before me, my personal representative shall distribute those items, as equally as possible, among my children who survive me. If no children survive me, these items shall be distributed as set forth in paragraph 2.3.

2.3 ALL OTHER ASSETS.

I give everything else I own to my spouse. If I am not married at the time I sign this will or if my spouse dies before me, I give these assets to my children and the descendants of any deceased child. If no spouse, children, or descendants of children survive me, I choose 1 of the following distribution clauses by signing my name on the line after that clause. If I sign on both lines, if I fail to sign on either line, or if I am not now married, these assets will go under distribution clause (b).

Distribution clause, if no spouse, children, or descendants of children survive me. (Select only 1)

(a) One-half to be distributed to my heirs as if I did not have a will, and one-half to be distributed to my spouse's heirs as if my spouse had died just after me without a will.

____
(Your signature)

(b) All to be distributed to my heirs as if I did not have a will.

____
(Your signature)

GUARDIAN, AND CONSERVATOR

Personal representatives, guardians, and conservators have a great deal of responsibility. The role of a personal representative is to collect your assets, pay debts and taxes from those assets, and distribute the remaining assets as directed in the will. A guardian is a person who will look after the physical well-being of a child. A conservator is a person who will manage a child's assets and make payments from those assets for the child's benefit. Select them carefully. Also, before you select them, ask them whether they are willing and able to serve.

3.1 PERSONAL REPRESENTATIVE. (Name at least 1)

I nominate ____
(Insert name of person or eligible financial institution)

of ____________________________ to serve as personal representative.
(Insert address)

If my first choice does not serve, I nominate __________________________

____

(Insert name of person or eligible financial institution)

of____________________________ to serve as personal representative.
(Insert address)

3.2 GUARDIAN AND CONSERVATOR.

Your spouse may die before you. Therefore, if you have a child under age 18, name an individual as guardian of the child and an individual or eligible financial institution as conservator of the child's assets. The guardian and the conservator may, but need not, be the same person.

If a guardian or conservator is needed for a child of

mine, I nominate ____
(Insert name of individual)

of ____ as guardian
(Insert address)

and

____
(Insert name of individual or eligible financial institution)

of____ to serve as conservator.
(Insert address)

If my first choice cannot serve, I nominate

____
(Insert name of individual)

of ____ as guardian
(Insert address)

and

____

(Insert name of individual or eligible financial institution)

of ____ to serve as conservator.
(Insert address)

3.3 BOND.

A bond is a form of insurance in case your personal representative or a conservator performs improperly and jeopardizes your assets. A bond is not required. You may choose whether you wish to require your personal representative and any conservator to serve with or without bond. Bond premiums would be paid out of your assets. (Select only 1)

(a) My personal representative and any conservator I have named shall serve with bond.

____

(Your signature)

(b) My personal representative and any conservator I have named shall serve without bond.

____

(Your signature)

3.4 DEFINITIONS AND ADDITIONAL CLAUSES.

Definitions and additional clauses found at the end of this form are part of this will.

I sign my name to this Michigan statutory will on ______________, 20_____.

____

(Your signature)

NOTICE REGARDING WITNESSES

You must use 2 adults as witnesses. It is preferable to have 3 adult witnesses. All the witnesses must observe you sign the will, have you tell them you signed the will, or have you tell them the will was signed at your direction in your presence.

STATEMENT OF WITNESSES

We sign below as witnesses, declaring that the individual who is making this will appears to be of sound mind and appears to be making this will freely, without duress, fraud, or undue influence, and that the individual making this will acknowledges that he or she has read the will, or has had it read to him or her, and understands the contents of this will.

____

(Print Name)

____

(Signature of witness)

____

(Address)

____

(City) (State) (Zip)

____

(Print name)

____

(Signature of witness)

____

(Address)

____

(City) (State) (Zip)

____

(Print name)

____

(Signature of witness)

____

(Address)

____

(City) (State) (Zip)

DEFINITIONS

The following definitions and rules of construction apply to this Michigan statutory will:

(a) "Assets" means all types of property you can own, such as real estate, stocks and bonds, bank accounts, business interests, furniture, and automobiles.

(b) "Descendants" means your children, grandchildren, and their descendants.

(c) "Descendants" or "children" includes individuals born or conceived during marriage, individuals legally adopted, and individuals born out of wedlock who would inherit if their parent died without a will.

(d) "Jointly held assets" means those assets to which ownership is transferred automatically upon the death of one of the owners to the remaining owner or owners.

(e) "Spouse" means your husband or wife at the time you sign this will.

(f) Whenever a distribution under a Michigan statutory will is to be made to an individual's descendants, the assets are to be divided into as many equal shares as there are then living descendants of the nearest degree of living descendants and deceased descendants of that same degree who leave living descendants. Each living descendant of the nearest degree shall receive 1 share. The remaining shares, if any, are combined and then divided in the same manner among the surviving descendants of the deceased descendants as if the surviving descendants who were allocated a share and their surviving descendants had predeceased the descendant. In this manner, all descendants who are in the same generation will take an equal share.

(g) "Heirs" means those persons who would have received your assets if you had died without a will, domiciled in Michigan, under the laws that are then in effect.

(h) "Person" includes individuals and institutions.

(i) Plural and singular words include each other, where appropriate.

(j) If a Michigan statutory will states that a person shall perform an act, the person is required to perform that act. If a Michigan statutory will states that a person may do an act, the person's decision to do or not to do the act shall be made in good faith exercise of the person's powers.

ADDITIONAL CLAUSES

Powers of personal representative

1. A personal representative has all powers of administration given by Michigan law to personal representatives and, to the extent

funds are not needed to meet debts and expenses currently payable and are not immediately distributable, the power to invest and reinvest the estate from time to time in accordance with the Michigan prudent investor rule. In dividing and distributing the estate, the personal representative may distribute partially or totally in kind, may determine the value of distributions in kind without reference to income tax bases, and may make non-prorata distributions.

2. The personal representative may distribute estate assets otherwise distributable to a minor beneficiary to the minor's conservator or, in amounts not exceeding $5,000.00 per year, either to the minor, if married; to a parent or another adult with whom the minor resides and who has the care, custody, or control of the minor; or to the guardian. The personal representative is free of liability and is discharged from further accountability for distributing assets in compliance with the provisions of this paragraph.

POWERS OF GUARDIAN AND CONSERVATOR

A guardian named in this will has the same authority with respect to the child as a parent having legal custody would have. A conservator named in this will has all of the powers conferred by law.

Witnesses

Michigan law requires that any will other than a holographic will must be signed by at least two disinterested individuals, each within a reasonable time after he or she witnessed the signing of the will or the testator's acknowledgment of his or signature on the will. This means that you can sign the will and then have the witnesses come in later and attest your signature. The better approach is to do the signing in their presence — together — and then have each sign as witness to your signing.

Witnesses should be at least age 18 and should include under their signature their legible printed name, address, and telephone number. If the will is contested in the future when you are no longer able to explain what happened, the witnesses may be called upon to confirm that each signed as witness to the will, that the other witness was there at the same time, and for any other information that he or she might recall about the circumstances of the will's execution. Witnesses are important for typed and printed wills for the obvious reason that anyone can print or type a document and try to forge a name on it. It has been done more times in history than can be counted. Holographic wills are an exception because it is more difficult to forge an entire document in a testator's own handwriting than it is a single signature.

One lawyer's anecdotal story illustrates the type of shenanigans that take place when it comes to wills. He was called out late at night by a client's son who asked him to come to the house because the client (the mother) was very ill and wanted the lawyer to witness her signing her new will and take it into his custody. "Couldn't this wait until morning?" the lawyer asked. "She insists it has to be you," said the son, "and I'm not sure she will last the night." The lawyer, having served the client for many years, went to the house and was ushered into the woman's bedroom, where he found her propped on her pillows, a document before her on the bed, and a pen in her hand.

The son said to him, "Mother is having trouble speaking now, but I will help her sign the will, and we can both witness it." Whereupon, the son took the mother's hand and started to guide it upon the paper. "Wait a moment," said the lawyer, and he spoke to his client, who did not answer. He stepped closer and reached for her wrist. The son attempted to interfere, but the lawyer pushed him away and sought a pulse. As you have now guessed, the mother had already passed away, and the son was attempting to get the new will signed posthumously, in hopes the lawyer would either be fooled or go along with it. Truth is stranger than fiction. Of course, the son could not have been a valid witness anyway because — as will be discussed further — he was named in the purported will. Whatever the mother might have intended about the new will, she died before signing it. Nor did she create an oral will, as will be further discussed.

Will: Uniform International Wills Act

Michigan recognizes wills made in foreign countries, subject to compliance with specific formalities of certification so that it will be recognized as valid. These formalities are stated in Michigan probate code 700.2953 as follows:

> "a) The will shall be made in writing, but does not need to be written by the testator personally. The will may be written in any language and may be written by hand or by any other means.
>
> (b) The testator shall declare in the presence of 2 witnesses and an authorized individual that the document is the testator's will and that he or she knows its contents. The testator need not inform the witnesses or the authorized person of the will's contents.
>
> (c) In the witnesses' and the authorized individual's presence, the testator shall sign the will or, if the testator has previously signed the will, shall acknowledge his or her signature.
>
> (d) If the testator is unable to sign the international will, the absence of the testator's signature does not affect the will's validity if the testator indicates the reason for the inability and the authorized individual makes note of the reason on the will. In such a case, it is permissible, but not required, for another individual present, including a witness or the authorized individual, to sign the testator's name at the testator's direction, which act the authorized individual shall also note on the will.
>
> (e) The witnesses and the authorized individual shall there and then attest the will by signing in the presence of the testator."

In addition, it is recommended that a will of multiple pages be signed on each page by the testator, witnesses, and authorized individual.

Michigan Probate Code 700.2955
International Will Certificate

The authorized individual shall attach to the will a certificate signed by the authorized individual establishing that the will complies with the requirements of this part for valid execution of an international will. The authorized individual shall keep a copy of the certificate and deliver another to the testator. The certificate must be in substantially the following form, except the provisions of the form that are optional provisions need only be included if the circumstances of the will render them applicable:

CERTIFICATE
(Convention of October 26, 1973)

1. I, ______________________________,
(Name, address and capacity)
a person authorized to act in connection with international wills

2. Certify that on ________ at ______________________
(Date) (Place)

3. (Testator) ______________________________
(Name, address, date and place of birth)
in my presence and that of the witnesses

4. (a) ______________________________
(Name, address, date and place of birth)

(b) ______________________________
(Name, address, date and place of birth)

has declared that the attached document is his (or her) will and that he (or she) knows the contents thereof.

5. I furthermore certify that:

6. (a) In my presence and in that of the witnesses (1) the testator has signed the will or has acknowledged his (or her) signature previously affixed. * following a declaration of the testator stating that he (or she) (2) was unable to sign his (or her) will for the following reason ______________________________,

I have mentioned this declaration on the will * and the signature has been affixed by

____

(Name and address)

7. (b) The witnesses and I have signed the will;

8. *(c) Each page of the will has been signed by

______________________________ and numbered;

9. (d) I have satisfied myself as to the identity of the testator and of the witnesses as designated above;

10. (e) The witnesses have met the conditions requisite to act as such according to the law under which I am acting;

11. *(f) The testator has requested me to include the following statement concerning the safekeeping of his (or her) will:

12. PLACE OF EXECUTION

13. DATE

14. SIGNATURE and, if necessary, **SEAL**

* to be completed if appropriate.

An "authorized person" to handle the above certificate in Michigan is a Michigan lawyer in good standing.

Changing Your Will – Codicils

You have made your will and it is done. Along comes a new idea; another child is born; new property is acquired or property is sold; a divorce occurs; a marriage happens; a death happens; or a loss occurs. Life changes. Whatever the reason, you decide you want to change something in your will, just one provision or part of it, or you just want to add something to it without changing the whole thing. A codicil is an addition you can write and attach to or put with your existing will. You may do this in Michigan by the holographic method — by handwriting it and signing and dating it, designating it as a codicil to your will. If it is not holographically prepared, then the codicil must meet the same requirements with witnesses as the full will. If there are multiple codicils, and they contradict each other, the most recently signed and dated codicil will be the provision that is considered valid.

Where to Keep Your Will

Keep your will in a safe place, but one where it can be found when you are no longer here. Many people deposit their will with their attorney who assisted in drafting it. This is not a bad practice, especially if the attorney or his or her firm is the legal fiduciary whom you wish to assist with the probate of your will. You could also keep the will in a home safe that is fireproof or with the person whom you have named as your executor or executrix of the will.

Beneficiaries, Debts, and Entitlements

Subject to certain limitations, you can leave your property and possessions to anyone you wish. If you are married and you disinherit your spouse, your spouse has rights under Michigan law to make a claim against the will for his or her statutory elective share of the estate. In this regard, a surviving spouse has options to consider, which are best discussed with a lawyer, as there are nuances that depend upon whether the surviving spouse is a widow or widower, whether the surviving spouse is living in Michigan at the time, the number of surviving children, and the desires of the surviving spouse. Most often, the surviving spouse receives what the spouse would be entitled to receive if the testator had died without a will, i.e., the surviving spouse's intestate share. The main point to understand is that disinheriting a lawful spouse will not be enforced if the spouse does not consent to be disinherited.

Similarly, children of the decedent can also make claims against a will that does not mention them. Omitted children and after-born children will be presumed to be an oversight. If you wish to disinherit one or more of your children, including any not yet born, it is best to expressly say so in the will, even though the words might sound harsh in black and white. Omission by silence might raise a question of mistake and open your intent to dispute. Wills have been challenged successfully by children appearing who were presumed dead, who were not known to exist, who were born after the will was prepared, or who were disinherited by simply not being named in it. What the testator intended about these children was not clear. Therefore, it was presumed the testator intended to include the child in the estate.

You can name entities and charities in your will, of course. When it comes to pets, be careful how you handle this in Michigan. If you make Fluffy a direct beneficiary, Fluffy is not a "person." One way is to name a person in your will as a beneficiary who gets ownership and possession of Fluffy, along with a sum of money for Fluffy's care. For obvious reasons, this needs to be someone you trust to care for Fluffy, someone with whom you have discussed this plan when you made your will. Also, you should have a contingency in the will for if you outlive Fluffy.

An even better approach is to set-up a pet trust for Fluffy, which is a mechanism recognized in Michigan. As the beneficiary of the trust, Fluffy can be cared for during her lifetime. The trust has a trustee named to ensure the pet's care and administer the funds placed in the trust. In determining the amount for the trust, such factors as the animal's expected life span and support needs — such as veterinary costs, grooming, medicine, food, and board — must be factored into the estimate. Discuss with your lawyer how to set-up a pet trust under Michigan law and endow it with sufficient funding.

Bequests to Minors

Money and property of any significant value left to children under age 18 will be controlled by Michigan's Uniform Transfers to Minors Act. If you do not name a specific person to be the custodian of the property for the child until the child reaches age 18, the child's "personal representative," who is the child's parent or guardian, will be the custodian of your bequest unless the court names a different person. You can also arrange in your will for property to be held in trust for a child until a later age. For this type of arrangement, you do not want to leave the details to chance. Hire a Michigan lawyer to assist you in drafting these provisions to ensure your wishes are carried out in the way you intend. You may be better advised to create a trust for a minor during your lifetime, or a pour-over testamentary trust, depending on your circumstances, timing, and the type of property or extent of wealth involved. By setting up the trust yourself, you exercise better control over the administration of the bequest.

Intestate in Michigan

Probate law does not permit a vacuum. If a person dies without a valid will, Michigan law provides how the person's possessions — his estate — will be divided. As mentioned, in simple terms, if there is a surviving spouse, all will go to the surviving spouse unless there are surviving children of the decedent who are not also the children of the surviving spouse. If there is at least one surviving child and surviving spouse, and the child is not the child of the surviving spouse, then the statute provides for a proportional division, which will change according to how many surviving children of the decedent are not related to the spouse. If there is no surviving spouse, but a surviving child — or parents, siblings, or other family members — then depending on the relationship of the survivors to the decedent and in what numbers, the estate will be divided among them as prescribed by statute. The court will not take into consideration anything else, such as charities, non-relatives, friends, or other relations that might have been important to the decedent, because Michigan law does not recognize such considerations or relationships, only next of kin.

Death Taxes

At present, Michigan does not have its own death tax scheme. It is allied with the federal tax scheme. Currently and through 2011, Michigan is not assessing death and inheritance taxes, but this is likely to change. Check the status of this point for yourself in the future, though, as you prepare your will and estate, because the Michigan legislature has been contemplating ways to recoup death tax revenues with new legislation.

How Your Will Might Be Challenged

By now, you have an idea of the ways someone may challenge your will if you have not closed the loopholes when you prepared it. The ways such challenges most often arise are:

1. The document filed with the court is not a valid holographic will because one or more of the following is missing: proper date, signature, or words indicating it is meant to be your last will and testament or substantive parts of it are not in your handwriting.

2. It is not a holographic will and, in addition to any of the above indicia of a will being missing, it is not simultaneously witnessed by at least two competent witnesses who are not "interested parties" in your will.

3. You were not of sound mind when you wrote it.

4. Some part or all of the will does not comply with Michigan law.

5. Someone who claims to be your biological offspring appears who is not mentioned in the will.

6. Someone appears who claims to be your lawful spouse who is not mentioned or is disinherited in the will.

7. Someone comes forward with a new will or codicil of a newer date.

8. The will is claimed to be a forgery or fraud.

9. Someone claims you were under coercion.

If the will first presented to the probate court meets all the basic legal requirements — original document, dated, intent or agreement to be a will demonstrated, disposal of property contained within, signature, and proper witnesses to the signature (if not a valid holographic will) — the court will presume the will to be valid until proved otherwise. The challenger can file another will or codicil for the court to consider and evaluate or can challenge the will itself, but the challenger must present evidence.

Perhaps the easiest challenge to a will is producing a more recent one that exhibits all the legal requirements, but where two wills are brought into question, it will often rest on the testimony of witnesses, and sometimes a handwriting expert, to determine which is the true will. The one of most recent date will be the controlling will. When you make a new will, you automatically revoke all prior wills. When you make a codicil to an existing will, you only revoke a provision of the will that you are changing, not the entire will, because you are not making an entire new will when you prepare a codicil.

You can look ahead to potential challenges and prepare your will to prevent those challenges from having any effect on your wishes by preparing your will, with the assistance of counsel, to ensure it expresses your intent and meets the statutory requirements of a will.

A Different Type of Will — Your Living Will in Michigan

A "living will" is not about dispersing your property and stating your final wishes at the time of your death. It is about having your own control over your body if accident or illness puts you in a medical situation in which it is difficult or impossible for you to speak for yourself in the moment. With a living will, a person can put in writing that he or she does not wish to be placed on life support systems if terminally ill or permanently unconscious (coma). The living will concept does not have the teeth of enforcement in all states. Michigan does not have a specific living will statute, but it does for the durable power of attorney for health care. Further, the State Bar of Michigan provides sample forms for three types of directives, indicating they will be binding in Michigan: living will, durable power of attorney for health care, and do not resuscitate (DNR) directive, as well as an anatomical gift designation. These forms can be found at the State Bar of Michigan's website **www.michbar.org/elderlaw/adpamphlet.cfm**.

Fishing Village in Michigan

CHAPTER 12

Keeping it Current

You have a will. All your trust documents are properly executed. Your brother has agreed to be your trustee, and your sister is his backup. Your cousin is your executor, with your aunt as backup. All guardians are on board. All your beneficiaries are alive and accounted for. Insurance policies are up to date. You have a living will and organ donation form in the hands of your doctor. All powers of attorney are ready, and your retirement is fully funded. Unfortunately, putting together a comprehensive estate plan is just the first step. The good news is that the final step is less time-consuming.

The final step is to review your plan once a year or whenever there is a significant change that will affect your plan or beneficiaries. If you schedule a review when you change the batteries in your smoke detectors on the first day of spring or at the end of summer, you will have time to implement any updates that will take advantage of any changes in tax laws before the end of the fiscal year. The regular discipline means you will be able to take care of little changes quickly instead of having to go through the arduous process of making many changes all at one time.

After the volume of work that went into this plan, it might seem that a once-a-year review is quick and easy, but for those who wish to wash their hands of the whole business, that might seem too frequent. Your perspective is relative, so following the advice of those who know is a good idea. Most estate planning professionals will tell you it is not a good idea to make many small changes throughout the year. It could get seriously expensive and complicated. A decision made in the midst of a difficult experience — such as eliminating a beneficiary from your estate — could result in a domino effect, with additional changes necessary, which will cost more time and stamina than you might have available. Change your mind again later, and the process starts all over.

The annual review sets a specific time for addressing issues that come up throughout the year. It also keeps your estate plan in the back of your mind. Just as you need to remember to change the oil in your car or the engine will blow up, you need to make changes to your estate plan or it will not work the way you want it to. Once your estate plan is in place, maintenance can be simple.

What Changes?

It is not difficult to imagine the implication of some common life changes. Marriage, divorce, death of a beneficiary, the birth of a child, or losing your job will mean obvious changes to an estate plan: changing beneficiaries, including/removing a spouse on ownership documents, and updating your name if you legally change it. Other changes are going to require some thought and planning in order to make the necessary adjustments to your original plan.

Property:

- You give away or sell property specified in a will or trust.
- A natural disaster destroys or causes serious damage to a piece of real estate.
- You acquire a substantial amount of new property.
- Your home is robbed, and property in your will is stolen.

Health:

- You or someone in your family is diagnosed with a life-threatening illness.
- You are hurt on the job.
- A parent becomes seriously ill and cannot afford medical care.
- The doctor gives you a clean bill of health, and you can go back to work.

Good news (with strings attached):

- Your daughter is accepted to Harvard but does not qualify for student loans.
- The adoption agency in Europe approved your five-year-old application, and you need to go pick up your son next week.
- Your trustee was transferred to Nepal with no set return date.
- Your wife received a promotion and you are moving to the West Coast, which is closer to her family.

Some of these situations could mean you need to take out a loan against your retirement savings, but others will involve the thoughtful work of choosing a new personal representative and getting the related documents up to date. Immediate needs ought to be addressed as they arise, such as naming a new trustee before heading to Europe to adopt your son, but some things can wait. Figuring out how to pay for a Harvard education and the implications it will have for your estate will take some time.

Check with the members of your estate-planning team to find out what kinds of changes they think ought to be addressed as quickly as possible, and what can wait. Establish how you will communicate these things — e-mail notes to an assistant or a signed original letter. Few finance-related companies will accept or execute directions left in a voice-mail message, but maybe a message telling your adviser that an e-mail is coming and asking her to call when it arrives will suffice.

Once you are clear about the information you need to collect, make sure that you are keeping track of those pieces of information throughout the year. Consolidate and organize the information that will make it easy for you and your estate-planning team to have what they need. Create a file folder, make a running list, or designate a desk in your drawer for estate-planning essentials.

Make a copy of the acceptance letter from Harvard, staple to the back a printout of the tuition and fee schedule you pulled from the website, and scribble notes to yourself for reference later: "Transfer stock from living trust? Sell time share?" If you are going to hand over documents to your lawyer or CPA, be sure to keep a copy for your files; if his gets lost or you need to discuss something over the phone, having a backup copy will make things simpler.

What Does "Maintenance" Look Like?

Your estate-planning team might be a group of two or 16 individuals in one or eight different companies. Regardless of their number, they are all likely to have an idea about how to coordinate your annual review, make changes, and handle documents. With that many people involved, the potential for disaster is only slightly limited by the fact that they all have a stake in making sure your plan remains intact and up to date. As the person with the estate, you need to decide what is most comfortable and reasonable for you.

A simple approach makes the most sense for something new; it will get complicated all by itself, so no need to help that along.

Make a list of each person in your estate-planning team along with their contact information, including company name and secondary contact. Then add the elements of your estate plan for which they are responsible.

The following is an example of how this contact sheet may look.

Pat Johnson, Attorney at law
(Primary contact)
Dewey Cheatum and Howe
1234 Jokester Lane, Suite 6789
New York, Michigan 55555
513-555-1234 – Office
513-558-1098 – Direct line
513-555-2345 – Fax
513-555-3456 – Mobile
513-555-4567 – Home/emergency

Gail Silver, Attorney at law
(Secondary contact)
Dewey Cheatum and Howe
1234 Jokester Lane, Suite 6789
New York, Michigan 55555
513-555-1234 – Office
513-555-9876 – Direct line
513-555-2345 – Fax
513-555-8765 – Mobile
513-555-7654 – Home/emergency

** If neither contact is available, call the main number and explain the situation. The receptionist will find an alternative contact for immediate assistance. **

Hours: M - F 8 a.m. - 6 p.m., Sat. - by appointment, Sun. - closed
Documents: Will, living will, and organ donation documents
Stored: Dewey's document vault

Once your list is compiled, look over all the contacts and decide who would make the best point person or coordinator among the group. This person will serve as the top of the phone tree; in the case of a need or emergency, you only have one person to call who will inform the rest, so you only have to say things once. Just like on a snow day, one parent has a short list of people to call to say that school is closed, and each of those people has a short list. That way, everyone finds out rather quickly that it is a day for sledding. In the case of your estate plan, if one meeting is preferred, then your point person will collect and prepare all the documents needed from each person on the team so that you do not have to run all over town. The person who takes on this responsibility might charge a fee for this work, but when you are short on time, the convenience is well worth the investment.

Next, you need to choose a date for that annual review. If you only have two people with whom to meet, you could schedule back-to-back appointments on the same day and take care of your work for the year. The timing of this review will depend as much on your goals for your estate plan as it will on the space in your calendar. If taxes are a primary concern, then schedule your review at a point in the year that will allow you to have enough time to review the changes and make and implement decisions to maximize your savings or minimize your payments. If trusts are a big part of your estate, then the same kind of review will be needed to address any changes in trust regulations.

The likelihood of having time to do a review at the end of the year might be unrealistic — trying to squeeze in the appointments necessary between holiday parties, shopping, visits by out-of-town family, and inclement weather in some parts of the country. But then spring is a busy time, too, with breaks in school schedules and getting ready for graduations and summer vacations. There are more uses of your time than you thought imaginable when it comes to setting up a review of your estate plan. Ask your advisers what they think.

Periodic updates each quarter might help define when the annual review ought to happen. If a new tax law is passed in February, then an update from your CPA in March will give you plenty of time to reach and consider the implications before the annual review you schedule for early September

— the kids are back in school and the holiday rush has not yet begun. This kind of attention to your plan throughout the year will make the annual sit-down less involved.

If you have your planners get in touch with you a month or two in advance of your meeting, in addition to reminding you that it is coming, this will allow you to give them some directions about documents that need to be prepared. Following are a few examples of what could be happening that would be important to pass along:

- Your daughter Elizabeth just had a baby — Jeremy Jason Wolf — so you want to create a trust just like the one you have for all the other grandchildren. He also needs to be added to your will.
- Grandma Sophie passed away unexpectedly the week after Jeremy arrived; something needs to be done about her trust for assisted living expenses, and you need to consider suggestions about what to do with it. She also needs to be taken out of your will, with Grandpa George as the new beneficiary for her bequests.
- Kelley dropped out of business school to pursue an arts training program — will her education trust be able to cover her expenses even though the apprenticeship-like institution is not accredited?

You could sit down and sign the necessary documents at your review. Some of your team members might regard the review as the time to go over all that information and follow up with the document signing later. Keeping your team in the loop about what is happening in your life is important so that they can manage your estate plan, but you need to make sure that communication, again, supports your estate-plan goals. An e-mail or phone call when something significant occurs might be essential. Then again, waiting might not make much difference to your plan; it could save you considerable hassle given the number of times you would have to make those contacts.

What to Go Over

You need to go over all elements of your estate plan. Until the documents and routine become familiar, it could be easy to forget some of them. The estate planning worksheets in Appendix A summarize the components of your estate plan, which might include:

Will
Living will
Organ donor form/card
Durable power of attorney
Medical power of attorney
Guardians for children
Guardians for others
Life insurance policies
Disability insurance policies
Other insurance policies
Trust: For children
Trust: For retirement
Trust: For charity ________________
Trust: For charity ________________
Trust: Living ____________________
Retirement: 401(k)/pension

You will also want to consider your executor and backup, trustees and their backups, and anything else that is people-related. The goal is to make sure your documents reflect your wishes so that after you are gone, no matter when that happens, your estate is disposed of the way you want. It also helps the people you leave behind, so you need to address with your estate-planning team how to make sure those things happen.

Your Desk

Federal law requires individuals and businesses to retain documentation that supports tax returns for a specific number of years. Anyone who has had to go through an audit learns the hard way that this is not merely a guideline. Estate-planning documents could be considered more important than your tax records because they are the legal record dictating the disposal of your property, and what happens to that directly affects the taxes paid by your estate and every one of your beneficiaries. Stuffing those things into a cubby of an over-stuffed, roll-top desk and forgetting about them is not wise. Imagine your family trying to find the name of your lawyer in such a mess.

How to organize your documents and information is a personal matter. One file folder of everything might suffice, whereas a separate folder for each estate-planning team member might work best. Or you might assign one folder per document so that the history of all changes is readily accessible. Whatever method you choose, be sure to include any information your family might need to access after your death. You should include the following information:

- **Contact information**: Company name, phone number, fax, e-mail address, and any other information that you use to manage these accounts
- **Payment information:** Account numbers, usual due dates, and method of payment for any bills — automatic deductions from your checking or savings, on-line bill payment via your bank, coupon book, and checks mailed
- **Debts/accounts:**
    - **Real estate:** Home mortgage, second mortgage, timeshare, vacation property, and investment property
    - **Loans:** Line of credit, signature loans, and credit cards
    - **Utilities:** Gas, electric, water, sewer, heating oil, telephone, cell phone, Internet service provider, and cable/satellite

- ▶ **Regular payments:** Car payment, insurance, automatic deposits into savings or other accounts, magazine subscriptions, and newspaper delivery

- **Resources:**

  - ▶ **Income:** Payroll checks, rental income, structured settlement, royalties, annuity payments, and retirement distributions
  - ▶ **Bank accounts:** Checking, savings, and certificates of deposit (CDs)
  - ▶ **Investments:** Money market accounts

The Essential Documents and Accounts Inventory worksheet in Appendix A will help you begin assembling this information. If you already keep individual file folders for these documents so that you have a place to put the stubs from the electric company or receipts from the company that delivers your heating oil, then indicate the name and location of the folder. Also, note if there is a monthly payment book or the electronic delivery of notices instead of traditional mail delivery.

For the truly meticulous, it would be a good idea to have a centralized place for the original paperwork created when an account was set up, correspondences, and any other historical documents. When an executor of an estate is contacted about an outstanding debt, having access to that kind of information could make his or her job much easier.

Unfortunately, this kind of consolidation also makes it easier for a thief or unscrupulous family member to gain access to your assets. For this reason, it is important to keep these documents in a secure location. A fire-resistant home safe or locking file cabinet will make the materials readily available to you, but a greater challenge for someone else.

• *Did You Know?* •

If you want to be buried instead of cremated after you are gone, you need to let your wishes be known. A former queen of England prepared every detail of her funeral, including the conveyance of her coffin to the church and who would be invited to have a seat in a pew.

Another royal, not held in high esteem at the palace, died unexpectedly, so a funeral had to be prepared fast. The good news is that just such a funeral plan was ready; the bad news was mostly for the former queen who planned it — all her work was going to be used by someone else.

Most people will not need a protocol book for their final arrangements, but having things done your way will require you to make your wishes known. Planning your own funeral could seem a bit morbid, but look at it this way: you plan your birthday party, so why not plan your last party, too?

One Last Motivator: Probate and You

One big reason to make sure your estate plan is up to date is probate court, even though it is no longer the nightmare it used to be. The probate process is designed to settle your debts and distribute your assets when the proper legal documents are not provided.

After your death, your executor is required to file your will with the probate court in the appropriate jurisdictions. If you have homes in two different states, this means filing the will with the probate court in each state. The laws in each state might be slightly different, but the process is fairly standard. The following are general laws relating to probate:

- If a person dies without a will, an administrator — or executor — is appointed by the judge. If the person dies with a will but does not use will alternatives, such as trusts, to distribute assets to beneficiaries, then the named executor guides the will through the court process.
- The court posts a notice of your death in the newspaper to notify creditors of your death, and Michigan allows for a period of four months for claims to be made against the estate. Once the defined window of time is closed, no more requests for payment will be considered.

- The executor/administrator notifies all beneficiaries and creditors of the estate that the administration of the will is going forward.

- The executor/administrator collects all the assets and prepares a list or inventory. Court approval must be sought to sell any assets in order to pay debts or make bequests.

- The executor/administrator reviews and pays all outstanding debts.

- The executor/administrator pays all taxes.

- The executor/administrator distributes the remaining assets according to the order of the court.

If the individual dies intestate, the court will designate heirs. If there is a will and the probate process is used to settle the estate, then the court can make orders about which of the beneficiaries receives what. If a particular asset that was identified as a bequest has to be sold to pay taxes, then the court might order that the beneficiary of that asset be given something else or that the person gets nothing.

Circumstances that influence the probate process do arise, and how each court in various states will handle these might be different. In the case of murder, most states, including Michigan, will not permit someone who intentionally kills a person to inherit any portion of the deceased person's estate; this includes receiving the proceeds from a life insurance policy, trust, or other arrangement.

In the case of adultery or abandonment, some intestate laws will not allow the spouse who cheated or deserted to inherit anything from the estate. The evidence needed to make the case for either situation varies. One distinction is clear in most states: a missing spouse is different from abandonment. A spouse who has not voluntarily moved out but is gone without any explanation can be declared missing. A period of years must pass — the minimum amount of time varies by state — before any legal action can be taken. Michigan has adopted the Federal Missing Persons Act, which presumes death when a person is missing for a continuous period of 12 months. The family can then request that a person be declared legally dead, making it possible to execute a will, receive insurance benefits, and proceed with other estate-related activities.

The advantage of probate court is that, if you have a feuding family or just do not care what happens to your belongings when you are gone, the state will take care of it for you. If either case is true, then you can save yourself the work of the annual review process. If you prefer to direct things yourself, the annual review process can prevent extensive probate involvement.

If you name a beneficiary for a trust or insurance policy, and that person declines the bequest or is dead, the secondary beneficiary will inherit. If you do not have a secondary beneficiary named, then the probate court will settle the matter. Any issues that you do not account for in your will, will alternatives, or other estate distribution activities will be settled by the probate court.

Taking a few hours each year to make sure your documents are in place and up to date is a small investment compared to the effort those who are left behind must expend.

Identity Theft

As you collect information about all your assets and liabilities and compile important personal information, it is important to be aware of safeguarding the related documentation. Identify theft is a quite real, dangerous threat. A person representing himself or herself as another individual is a crime that can be prevented. When you do not think like a criminal, it can be difficult to figure out what you need to do to protect yourself.

Some of the ways in which a skilled identity thief will steal your information might surprise you. The following are ways to consider:

- **Change of address:** By submitting a change of address card with the United States Postal Service (USPS), the thief will send your mail to a location where he or she can get at it without suspicion.
- **Stealing:** Taking mail out of your mailbox is a bit more risky, but it does happen. Completing and returning pre-approved credit cards, with a change of address, is just one way your mail can be used to steal your identity (along with stealing your wallet, personal records from an employer, or offering bribes to employees who have access to sell your information).
- **Dumpster diving:** This is the act of looking through trash to find bills or bank statements with account information or any personal information that might be useful in the act of stealing someone's identity, such as a social security number, mother's maiden name, or personal identification number (PIN). This is not considered theft; the U.S. Supreme Court has ruled that anything left out for trash collection is in the public domain.
- **Skimming:** This is accomplished by using a special high-tech storage device that electronically "grabs" your account number and other personal information when a store computer is processing your credit card purchase/transaction.
- **Phishing**: A thief will pretend to represent a bank, some other financial institution, or a legitimate business in the form of an e-mail or as a pop-up communication when you visit a website. These communications will ask you to verify or correct information provided and then ask for additional personal information.

Avoiding identity theft

If you want to avoid being robbed on the street, there are some common-sense things you can do without going to a "How Not to Get Mugged" class. Do not walk alone in a strange neighborhood at night, and only park in brightly lit parking lots. Like these obvious behaviors, there are some obvious things people do that help prevent identify theft, such as cutting up old credit cards instead of throwing them into the trash intact. But if you throw all the pieces into the same garbage bag, a thief can reassemble the pieces and make Internet purchases because he will have access to the security code on the back of the card.

Through the unfortunate experiences of those who have had their credit rating destroyed, among other unfortunate consequences, the methods of identity thieves are no longer a secret. There are many things you can do to avoid being robbed of your good name.

The first and most important thing is awareness: Pay attention to what you are doing with your personal information. If you are scribbling notes about the accounts you need to look up and then jot them down on a piece of paper so that you can enter them into a spreadsheet, do not throw that paper into the trash.

Create a pile or special trash can for "personal info." Put anything that needs to be disposed of in that one place, such as old utility bills, bank statements from an account you closed ten years ago, or statements from your insurance company telling you that a reimbursement has been made to your primary-care physician. Then choose a method for making those documents unreadable.

Invest in a small, crosscut shredder — scraps of paper can be reassembled like a puzzle. Remember the news clips of federal investigators hauling out bags of shredded documents from a national corporation under investigation? If your documents are not old and dusty, call your local animal shelter and ask whether they can use shredded paper for litter boxes.

It is not very likely a thief is going to want to go through that much effort to go through your documents once the cats, dogs, or guinea pigs are done with them. Most shredders will also destroy credit cards; make sure you do not mix your plastic with paper going to the shelter. If you want to be super-safe with your credit card bits, separate the plastic bits into several different trash cans and dispose of them at different times.

Burning paper until it is a powdery ash also works well. Some other ways to prevent identity theft are equally simple, once you have them in mind.

- Never give out personal information to a stranger over the telephone or via blind mailers. If you want to register an appliance or request more information from a company, call them. Do not fill out a postcard that asks for your e-mail address, birth date, or other personal data that can be read and copied by anyone who sees it.

Electronic communications should not be considered secure — they can be intercepted or read by someone other than your intended audience.

- If a delivery person says he is with the United States Postal Service (USPS) but is stopping by to drop off a package for his buddy on his way home after changing out of his uniform, refuse the package and tell him your usual letter carrier can come back tomorrow in uniform, and you will sign for it then. If that feels like being paranoid and untrusting, that is all right. You would not give your child to a stranger, so do not give yourself either, in the form of your personal information.

Be on the lookout

First and foremost, this means to protect any official documents or written materials — such as the completed worksheets from this book — so that nobody has access to them unless you grant them permission. A locking file cabinet with a limited number of keys that are not numbered is one option. Standard file cabinets, like the ones you can get from a large manufacturer, have a number written on the lock. If you lose the key, you can give them that number and a few dollars, and they will send a replacement, but they will do the same for a thief, no questions asked.

A fire-resistant safe or lock box that you can store at home will also work. Those safes are not fireproof, meaning whatever is inside will not necessarily survive in any fire. Fire-resistant means what is inside will be protected for a number of hours before the safe itself gets so hot that flammable material will catch fire and disintegrate. Portable boxes can also be stolen. None of this means you should not bother with these options, it just means you should be aware of the limitations of your choices.

Other choices you have for protection are being on the lookout for unusual problems:

- You are denied credit when you think your credit rating is sound.
- Bills or other information, such as letters or warranty offers, arrive for purchases you did not make.
- Bills that come at the same time every month or related to a specific purchase do not arrive as anticipated.

- Credit cards or account statements for which you did not apply are delivered.

If any of these things happen, investigate. Along those same lines, request a copy of your credit report on a regular basis, at least once a year, and check it for unusual activity; immediately follow up on anything that is suspicious. Federal law now requires nationwide credit reporting agencies to provide one free copy of your credit report each year, upon request. Visit **www.annualcreditreport.com** or call 877-322-8228 and request your free report. You can also write to:

Annual Credit Report Request Service
PO Box 105281
Atlanta, GA 30348-5281

Review any statements you get about existing accounts — credit card, checking, savings, money market — and see whether there is anything out of place. If something is wrong, or some vital information is stolen, act immediately.

Close any accounts that have been set up in your name but not by your doing or any account of yours that has been meddled with. Report the trouble immediately to your local police by filing a police report. Prepare an ID Theft Affidavit with the Federal Trade Commission, available via **www.ftc.gov.theft**, or report it via telephone at 877-ID-THEFT (438-4338) or TTY 866-653-4261. Traditional mail is also an option:

Identity Theft Clearinghouse
Federal Trade Commission
Washington, D.C. 20580

You can also place a "fraud alert" on your credit report; this instructs creditors to follow specific procedures before a new account is opened in your name. They will also follow these procedures when a change of personal information is requested. Before any action is taken, you can receive a phone call that will require the verification of a combination of specific personal information that would be difficult for a thief to have all at one time. There are only a few national credit reporting companies, so calling one company will let the others know that an alert has been requested — no need for you to call all three.

- Treat your social security number like gold; guard it the same way you would a gold coin. Do not carry your social security card in your wallet or purse, and never write it on a check. Only provide it when absolutely necessary, and then only to someone you have verified as an authorized agent for the company with whom you share it.
- Passwords for any account need to be unusual — do not use the birth dates of your children, your wedding anniversary, any portion of your social security number, or your telephone number. Some of that information is easy to obtain through public records requests, and it will provide open access to your accounts.
- Never communicate personal information via e-mail. If you need to get the information to someone quickly, call and leave a message in a private voice mail box or send a fax to a confidential location where the information will not be handled by many people. If e-mail is a necessary means for communicating, never send complete information in one e-mail: send most of your social security number in one e-mail and send the last four digits in a second e-mail. Same with account numbers — even better is to e-mail part and call with the remainder.

Equifax: 800-525-6285
Experian: 800-397-3742
TransUnion: 800-680-7289

Identity theft is a threat that ought to be taken seriously. Educate yourself and your family, and you will reduce your chances of being victimized.

Additional resources:

- About identity theft:
  - Federal Trade Commission: **www.ftc.gov/idtheft**
  - Identity Theft Resource Center: **www.idtheftcenter.org**
  - Social Security Administration: **www.socialsecurity.gov/pubs/10064.pdf**

- For victims of identity theft:
  - Privacy Rights Clearinghouse: **www.privacyrights.org**
  - Office of Justice Programs, Office for Victims of Crimes (OVC): **www.ojp.usdoj.gov/ovc/help/it.htm**

View of Detroit, Michigan skyline from Windsor, Ontario

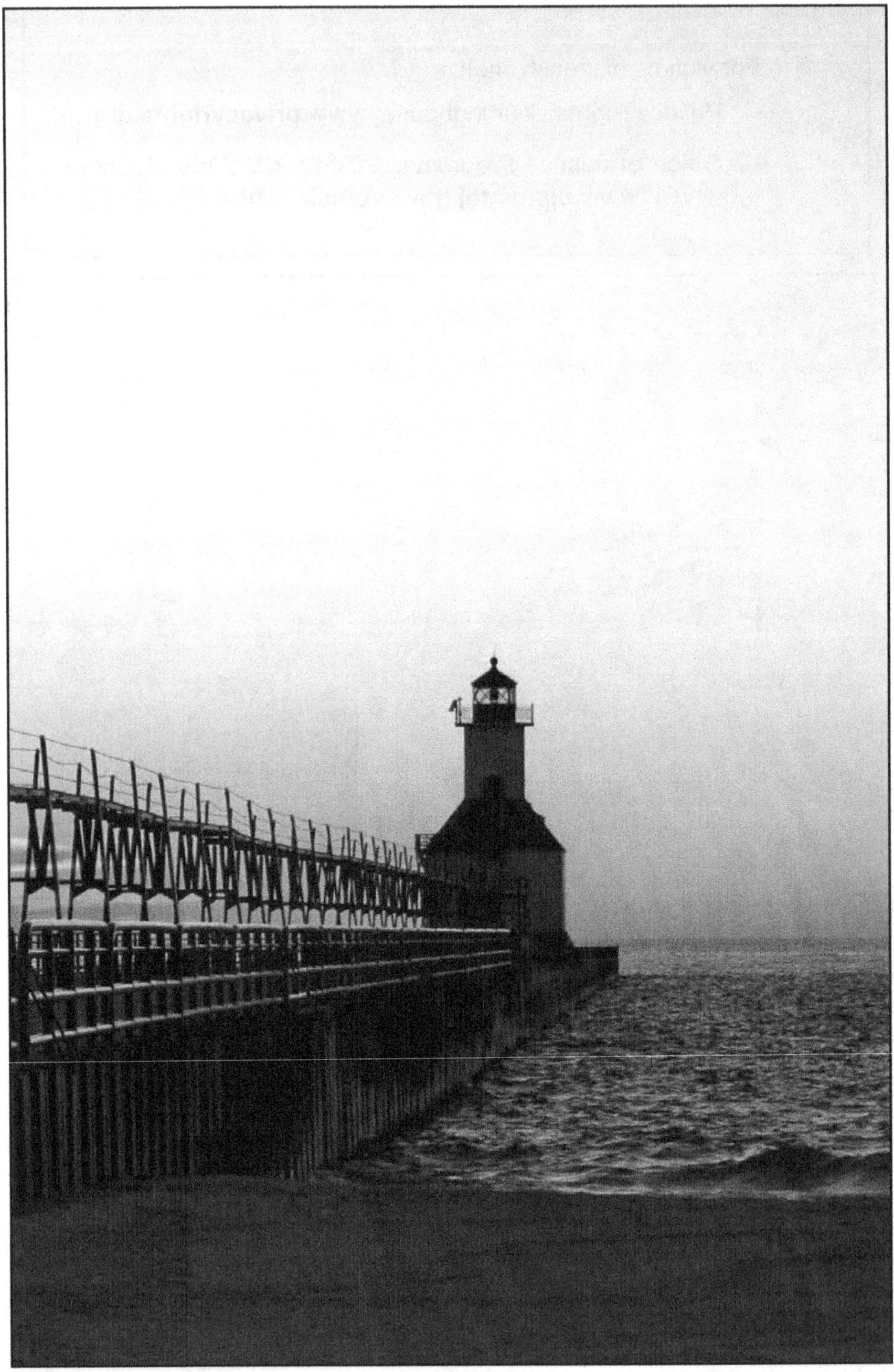

St Joseph North Pier Lighthouse, Michigan

CONCLUSION

Congratulations: you have an estate to plan. It turns out that you do not have to be rich, famous, or pompous to have the kind of resources that make it necessary to plan for the future.

The single most important thing you can do now is to create an estate plan. Even if you have done all the exercises in this book, you know there is much more work to do. The work that is necessary to move from where you are now to the point where you are scheduling regular annual meetings with estate professionals might seem a monumental task. But the good news is that it can be done. You have enough information to ask informed questions and begin to narrow down this huge idea of estate planning into your goals, will, and trusts.

The need to create your own definitions is why you did not find sample wills, a standard trust document, or an annuity template in these pages; it is counterproductive. Trying to shoehorn your information into a prescribed form supports a cookie-cutter approach to something that is highly personal — you are the one who loses with that kind of approach. The things you want to accomplish with the results of your years of hard work are not going to be like those of your brother Ben or your sister Sally. There will always be similarities, which is why books like this exist, but they need to serve as a place to begin, not end.

Customization takes time and stirs up considerable emotion, maybe even issues you would rather not face. Take your time and get the help you need with all of it. If you set your own pace and find people with whom you are comfortable, you will avoid unnecessary frustration, upset, and expense.

This is a big commitment, but when compared to the commitments it took to get to the point where you need to consider estate planning, this is a manageable process.

Build in some fun to get yourself through the difficult things. Every time you reach a milestone, like completing your will, treat yourself to a dinner out, or spend a day lounging under a tree reading a book. And always remind yourself of the gifts you give that cannot be delineated in writing — your wish to make your departure less burdensome, your thoughtfulness, and your love for the people in your life are all communicated through the effort of this work.

Appendix A:

Estate-Planning Worksheets

Your Estate in Black and White – Estate-Planning Inventory

Page 1

Name: ____________________ Birth:____________ SSN:________________

Spouse: ____________________ Birth:____________ SSN:________________

Primary address: ______________________________ # of Minors:________

Child: ____________________ Birth:____________ SSN:________________

Child: ____________________ Birth:____________ SSN:________________

Guardian of:________________ Birth:____________ SSN:________________

ASSETS				
Real estate: ***primary residence, vacation home, land***				
Address/ description	**Ownership**	**Mortgage(s)**	**Purchase price/year**	**Current value**

Automobile(s)				
Year	**Make**	**Model**	**Ownership**	**Current value**

Accounts: ***checking, savings, certificate of deposit, brokerage***			
Type	**Beneficiary(ies)**	**Account #**	**Current value**

Life insurance				
Company	**Insured**	**Beneficiary(ies)**	**Ownership**	**Face value**

Retirement: 401(k), ***IRA, Roth IRA, Keogh, pension, profit sharing, social security***				
Plan	**Ownership**	**Beneficiary(ies)**	**Vested year/%**	**Current value**

Other financial assets: ***stocks, bond, inheritance, structured settlement, rent payments***			
Type	**Beneficiary(ies)**	**Ownership**	**Current value**

Personal property: ***boat/jet ski, jewelry, artwork, antiques, collectibles, household contents, etc.***			
Type	**Value**	**Purchase year**	**Current value**

Page 2

ADDITIONAL ASSETS			
List all the things that did not fit on Page 1 of the inventory sheet:			
Type	**Value**	**Purchase year**	**Current value**

Value of all assets: $________________________

Total assets: $________________________

LIABILITIES			
First mortgage, second mortgage, line of credit, car loan, and credit card balance, for example			
Type	**Ownership**	**Due/payoff year**	**Current value**

Total liabilities $________________________

Total assets $________________________

Total liabilities $____________________

Total net worth $____________________

Prioritization

This is about making choices regarding what you can and cannot do with your estate. Choose six key values. These are the values or qualities to which you are attracted:

1	
2	
3	
4	
5	
6	

Then add the one key value to orient your life around: ________________

____

Now list all the things you would like to accomplish with your estate planning and connect those with your highest values: If more than one value is accomplished, note that.

		Goals	Value
1	$5K	Leave a substantial amount of money to cat shelter	Community involvement
2	$50K/ea	Education funds for niece and nephews	Education
3	$		
4	$		
5	$		
6	$		
7	$		
8	$		
9	$		
10	$		
11	$		

After you have completed your list of goals, place an approximate dollar value for the gift you would like to leave in the left-hand margin. Use a range if you are not sure.

Total gifts: $_______________________

Match this up against the *Estate-Planning Inventory* worksheet and see how close the dollar amounts are. If the numbers are nowhere near each other, then you might need to consider investing to build up your estate or changing the priorities in your list.

If they are close, consider what decisions need to be made to make a cash contribution, the transfer of real estate, or the value of property. If you list $500,000 in cash, are you willing or able to sell your house to come up with the money? Could you donate your house to a charitable institution in place of a cash donation? Would your family contest your will and challenge your wishes if the house has been in the family for generations? These are the details you need to discuss with your estate planner.

Who, What, How, and When

After you decide the people and organizations to receive a bequest, take a moment to write out your list. This will be useful when you sit down with your estate-planning team to finalize the paperwork and implementation of your estate plan. Leave any places blank if you are unsure.

Who/ relationship	What	How	When	Special circumstances
Jeanine/niece	*$50,000 + books ($10K value)*	*Trust (bequest)*	*2008*	*Will*
Cat shelter/charity	*$5,000*	*Bequest*	*2010*	*Will*
Me/Danny	*$250,000*	*Living trust/bequest*	*2008*	*Will*

Essential Documents and Accounts Inventory

Life will go on after you die, and handling your estate will likely fall to people who are mired in grief. To make it easier to find and deal with the accounts and obligations you leave behind, consolidate as much information as possible. This worksheet is a place to begin compiling that data.

This information will also be helpful to have when you meet with your estate planner.

DEBTS
Mortgage
Company name:
Account number:
Contact:
Phone number:

E-mail address:
Payment amount:
Usual due date:
Method of payment: *
PIN:
Second mortgage
Company name:
Account number:
Contact:
Phone number:
E-mail address:
Payment amount:
Usual due date:
Method of payment: *
PIN:
Timeshare: mortgage information
Company name:
Account number:
Contact:
Phone number:
E-mail address:
Payment amount:
Usual due date:
Method of payment: *
PIN:
Vacation property: mortgage information
Company name:
Account number:
Contact:
Phone number:

E-mail address:
Payment amount:
Usual due date:
Method of payment: *
PIN:
Loans: home equity
Company name:
Account number:
Contact:
Phone number:
E-mail address:
Payment amount:
Usual due date:
Method of payment: *
PIN:
Loans: line of credit
Company name:
Account number:
Contact:
E-mail address:
Payment amount:
Usual due date:
Method of payment: *
PIN:
Loans: signature
Company name
Account number:
Contact:
Phone number:
E-mail address:

Payment amount:
Usual due date:
Method of payment: *
PIN:
Loans: student/college tuition
Company name:
Account number:
Contact:
E-mail address:
Payment amount:
Usual due date:
Method of payment: *
PIN:
Loans: automobile
Company name:
Account number:
Contact:
E-mail address:
Payment amount:
Usual due date:
Method of payment: *
PIN:
Loans: other (e.g., boat or second car)
Company name:
Account number:
Contact:
E-mail address:
Payment amount:
Usual due date:
Method of payment: *
PIN:

Credit card 1
Company name:
Account number:
Contact:
E-mail address:
Payment amount:
Usual due date:
Method of payment: *
PIN:
Credit card 2
Company name:
Account number:
Contact:
E-mail address:
Payment amount:
Usual due date:
Method of payment: *
PIN:
Credit card 3
Company name:
Account number:
Contact:
E-mail address:
Payment amount:
Usual due date:
Method of payment: *
PIN:
Other: account 1
Company name:
Account number:
Contact:

E-mail address:
Payment amount:
Usual due date:
Method of payment: *
PIN:
Other: account 2
Company name:
Account number:
Contact:
Phone number:
E-mail address:
Payment amount:
Usual due date:
Method of payment: *
PIN:
Other: account 3
Company name:
Account number:
Contact:
Phone number:
E-mail address:
Payment amount:
Usual due date:
Method of payment: *
PIN:
LIVING EXPENSES
Gas and electric
Company name:
Account number:
Contact:
Phone number:

E-mail address:
Payment amount:
Usual due date:
Method of payment: *
PIN
Water and sewer (or septic)
Company name:
Account number:
Contact:
Phone number:
E-mail address:
Payment amount:
Usual due date:
Method of payment: *
PIN:
Telephone
Company name:
Account number:
Contact:
Phone number:
E-mail address:
Payment amount:
Usual due date:
Method of payment: *
PIN:
Heating oil
Company name:
Account number:
Contact:
Phone number:

E-mail address:
Payment amount:
PIN:
Internet service provider (ISP)
Company name:
Account number:
Contact:
Phone number:
E-mail address:
Payment amount:
Usual due date:
Method of payment: *
PIN:
Cable/satellite television service
Company name:
Account number:
Contact:
E-mail address:
Payment amount:
Usual due date:
Method of payment: *
PIN:
Other: account 1
Company name:
Account number:
Contact:
Phone number:
E-mail address:
Payment amount:
Usual due date:

Method of payment: *
PIN:
Other: account 2
Company name:
Account number:
Contact:
Phone number:
E-mail address:
Payment amount:
Usual due date:
Method of payment: *
PIN:
OTHER REGULAR PAYMENTS
Insurance: life – policy 1
Company name:
Account number:
Contact:
E-mail address:
Payment amount:
Usual due date:
Method of payment: *
PIN:
Insurance: life – policy 2
Company name:
Account number:
Contact:
Phone number:
E-mail address:
Payment amount:
Usual due date:

Method of payment: *
PIN:
Insurance: life – disability (long/short-term)
Company name:
Account number:
Contact
Phone number:
E-mail address:
Payment amount:
Usual due date:
Method of payment: *
PIN:
Insurance: homeowner's/renter's
Company name:
Account number:
Contact:
Phone number:
E-mail address:
Payment amount:
Usual due date:
Method of payment: *
PIN:
Insurance: car – policy 1
Company name:
Account number:
Contact:
Phone number:
E-mail address:
Payment amount:
Usual due date:

Method of payment: *
PIN:
Insurance: car – policy 2
Company name:
Account number:
Contact:
Phone number:
E-mail address:
Payment amount:
Usual due date:
Method of payment: *
PIN:
Newspaper: subscription 1
Company name:
Account number:
Contact:
Phone number:
E-mail address:
Payment amount:
Usual due date:
Method of payment: *
PIN:
Newspaper: subscription 2
Company name:
Account number:
Contact:
Phone number:
E-mail address:
Payment amount:
Usual due date:

Method of payment: *
PIN:
Magazine: subscription 1
Company name:
Account number:
Contact:
Phone number:
E-mail address:
Payment amount:
Usual due date:
Method of payment: *
PIN
Magazine: subscription 2
Company name:
Account number:
Contact:
Phone number:
E-mail address:
Payment amount:
Usual due date:
Method of payment: *
PIN:
Magazine: subscription 3
Company name:
Account number:
Contact:
Phone number:
E-mail address:
Payment amount:
Usual due date:

Method of payment: *
PIN:
Other: account 1
Company name:
Account number:
Contact:
Phone number:
E-mail address:
Payment amount:
Usual due date:
Method of payment: *
PIN:
Other: account 2
Company name:
Account number:
Contact:
Phone number:
E-mail address:
Payment amount:
Usual due date:
Method of payment: *
PIN:
INCOME
Payroll check 1
Company name:
Account number:
Contact:
Phone number:
E-mail address:
Check amount:

Pay day/dates:
Method of payment: *
(* check, direct deposit, cash, other)
Additional important information:
Payroll check 2
Company name:
Account number:
Contact:
Phone number:
E-mail address:
Check amount:
Pay day/dates:
Method of payment: *
(* check, direct deposit, cash, other)
Additional important information:
Structured settlement
Company name:
Account number:
Contact:
Phone number:
E-mail address:
Check amount:
Pay day/dates:
Method of payment: *
(* check, direct deposit, cash, other)
Additional important information:

Royalty payment 1
Company name:
Account number:
Contact:
Phone number:
E-mail address:
Check amount:
Pay day/dates:
Method of payment: *
(* check, direct deposit, cash, other)
Additional important information:
Royalty payment 2
Company name:
Account number:
Contact:
Phone number:
E-mail address:
Check amount:
Pay day/dates:
(* check, direct deposit, cash, other)
Method of payment: *
Additional important information:
Annuity payment 1
Company name:

Account number:
Contact:
Phone number:
E-mail address:
Check amount:
Pay day/dates:
(* check, direct deposit, cash, other)
Additional important information:
Annuity payment 2
Company name:
Account number:
Contact:
Phone number:
E-mail address:
Check amount:
Pay day/dates:
Method of payment: *
(* check, direct deposit, cash, other)
Additional important information:
Retirement distribution: plan 1
Company name:
Account number:
Contact:
Phone number:
E-mail address:
Check amount:

Pay day/dates:
Method of payment: *
(* check, direct deposit, cash, other)
Additional important information:
Retirement distribution: plan 2
Company name:
Account number:
Contact:
Phone number:
E-mail address:
Check amount:
Pay day/dates:
Method of payment: *
(* check, direct deposit, cash, other)
Additional important information:
Rental property 1
Company name:
Account number:
Contact:
Phone number:
E-mail address:
Check amount:
Pay day/dates:
Method of payment: *
(* check, direct deposit, cash, other)
Additional important information:

Rental property 2
Company name:
Account number:
Contact:
Phone number:
E-mail address:
Check amount:
Pay day/dates:
Method of payment: *
(* check, direct deposit, cash, other)
Additional important information:
FINANCIAL RESOURCES
Checking: account 1
Financial institution:
Account number:
Contact:
Phone number:
E-mail address:
Balance:
Date:
PIN:
Additional important information:
Checking: account 2
Financial institution:

Account number:
Contact:
Phone number:
E-mail address:
Balance:
Date:
PIN:
Additional important information:
Savings: account 1
Financial institution:
Account number:
Contact:
Phone number:
E-mail address:
Balance:
Date:
PIN:
Additional important information:
Savings: account 2
Financial institution:
Account number:
Contact:
Phone number:
E-mail address:
Balance:
Date:

PIN:
Additional important information:
Certificate of deposit: account 1
Financial institution:
Account number:
Contact:
Phone number:
E-mail address:
Balance:
Date:
PIN:
Additional important information:
Certificate of deposit: account 2
Financial institution:
Account number:
Contact:
Phone number:
E-mail address:
Balance:
Date:
PIN:
Additional important information:
Money market fund: account 1
Financial institution:

Account number:
Contact:
Phone number:
E-mail address:
Balance:
Date:
PIN:
Additional important information:
Money market fund: account 2
Financial institution:
Account number:
Contact:
Phone number:
E-mail address:
Balance
Date:
PIN:
Additional important information:
Other: account 1
Financial institution:
Account number:
Contact:
Phone number:
E-mail address:
Balance:
Date:

PIN:
Additional important information:
Other: account 2
Financial institution:
Account number:
Contact:
Phone number:
E-mail address:
Balance:
Date:
PIN:
Additional important information:

Anything that did not fit into a predetermined category:

____

____

____

____

____

____

____

Party Planning with an Unusual Twist

Whether you prefer a traditional, dignified ceremony or an occasion that is a more personal reflection of how you lived your life, the arrangements for the last event you will attend on earth can be up to you. However, you need to make the necessary arrangements, or direct others to do as you wish. *This is not a legally binding document; a lawyer will need to be consulted for the correct language and paperwork.*

Check all that apply — leave blank those things you do not want — and provide any details that are needed.

Your body:

☐ I want my body to be donated to medicine and used for the following purposes:____

____

☐ Release the final report, including all test results, to my executor/personal representative: ___________________________

____

____

☐ Conduct a post-mortem examination if the following circumstances occur:____

____

____

☐ Cremate my remains, and disposal of my ashes should be conducted as follows:____

____

____

☐ I request a burial to take place in this way:

____

____

____

Your service:

☐ I want a memorial service without a casket.

☐ I want a funeral without a casket.

☐ Memorial service with a casket conducted in the following manner:

☐ Closed

☐ Open

☐ Funeral home/mortuary:

Address: ____

____

Phone: ____

Arrangements on file under the name of: ______________________

____

☐ I would like a funeral service conducted in the following manner:

Place of worship: ______________________________________

Address: ____

Phone: ____

Presiding clergy: ______________________________________

Soloist: ____

Hymns: ____

____

____

Musical selections: ____________________________________

____

____

Musical instruments: ____________________________

____

____

Scripture, poem(s), and other materials to be included:

____

Other instructions:

____

____

____

____

Memorial gifts should be suggested for the following:

____

____

____

Other information: __________________________________

____

____

____

____

Signed: ________________________________Date:__________

Estate Plan Summary Sheet

There are many components that can go into an estate plan, but there are some basic documents that most people have. This is a brief inventory that can serve as a checklist for making sure you get the things done that you need to accomplish.

Use the blank lines to add other documents, such as a prenuptial agreement, that will affect your estate plan.

Estate plan components:	Deadline	Done on:	Notes:
Estate plan summary sheet			
Will			
Living will			
Organ donor form/card			
Durable power of attorney			
Medical power of attorney			
Guardians for children			
Guardians for others			
Life insurance policies			
Trust: For children			
Trust: For retirement			
Trust: For charity ________			
Trust: For charity ________			
Trust: Living ____________			
Retirement: 401(k)/pension ____________________ ____________________ ____________________ ____________________			

Use the notes sections as reminders for additional information that is needed before the next review. For example, write "Get name of Peace Center lawyer" to make sure you have a contact for the charitable trust documents that might need to get to the organization.

Annual To-do List

Once your estate plan is complete, this list will need to be customized to include each component.

Use the blank lines to add other documents, such as a prenuptial agreement, that will affect your estate plan.

Estate plan pieces:	Meeting date:	Changes needed:
Estate plan summary sheet		
Will		
Living will		
Organ donor form/card		
Durable power of attorney		
Medical power of attorney		
Guardians for children		
Guardians for others		
Life insurance policies		
Trust – ______________		
Trust – ______________		
Trust – ______________		
Trust – ______________		
Retirement – __________		
Retirement – __________		

Appendix B:

Glossary of Terms

#s

401(k) Plan — Named after the IRS code number defining this kind of plan, this retirement savings plan allows contributions to be made automatically by your employer via deductions from your paycheck, pretax. This plan only applies to for-profit businesses.

403(b) Plan — This is the 401(k) equivalent for not-for-profit entities and is named after the IRS code number defining this kind of retirement savings plan. It allows contributions to be made automatically by your employer via deductions from your paycheck, pretax.

A

Adeemed — The status given to a will if property is missing from your estate that is specifically named in the will.

Ademption Statute — State law governing the distribution of property in an estate if items are missing or adeemed.

Administrator — If you die without a will, the court appoints an individual, normally a spouse or child, who will serve in the same capacity as an executor. That person will handle all the estate paperwork, prepare a list of assets, deal with likely heirs, handle claims from creditors, make payments on outstanding debt, and handlc other estate-related matters.

Annuity — A retirement investment account that you create by contributing a specific amount of money over a predetermined period of time; there will be a fixed rate of return for a number of years.

- **Variable Annuity** — A retirement investment account that you create by contributing a specific amount of money over a predetermined period of time; the funds are invested in the stock market, so the return depends on how well or poorly the economy does.

Antilapse — The status of a will if a beneficiary in your will dies before you do.

Antilapse Statute — State law that dictates the state will intervene if the property in a will exists, but the beneficiary is no longer alive, and no contingent beneficiary is named.

Appointment Clause — A giving clause in your will that identifies the person who will manage your estate.

Asset — Anything a person owns or is owed; this can be money, real estate, investments, or any other tangible property.

Automobile Insurance — The exchange of premiums for a guaranteed payment to cover the damage or loss of a motor vehicle. Medical and liability coverage can also be included.

B

Bargain Sale — The sale of a piece of property to a charity at a rate that is below the fair market value. The difference between the amount paid and actual value is the amount of the gift.

Beneficiary — The individual(s) or group(s) that will receive the property in a will or trust. This can be a single person (a nephew), a group of people (all grandchildren), one group (Stray Cat Rescue, Inc.), several groups (all community councils in your city), or a combination of any of these.

Beneficial Title, or **Equitable Title** — The right of a person or institution to take possession of or benefit from the property in a trust.

Bequest — A legacy or gift given by a person to another person or entity through a last will and testament after the giver dies.

Burial Trust — Provides the funds necessary to cover the cost of your burial (or cremation) arrangements; this can be a revocable trust, but after your death, it becomes irrevocable, and the trust cannot be used for anything else.

Bypass Trust — This trust will transfer property to someone other than your spouse, such as a child or grandchild, but will allow him or her to still benefit from the property in the trust.

C

Certified Public Accountant (CPA) — A person who has gone through professional training and meets state requirements for both education and work experience, passed a national accounting exam, and met other licensing requirements to perform the tasks of accounting such as performing audits, preparing tax returns, and giving advice to their clients — individuals or businesses — on financial matters. Accountants can also specialize in various aspects of financial estate matters such as trusts, annuities, and estate tax law. However, they also serve as estate-planning specialists who can help you consider all financial decisions.

Charitable Trust — A method for giving charitable institutions gifts, including regular support on a time-release basis, that is tax-free for the donor.

Charitable Remainder Trust — Gives gifts of interest income that are paid to specific beneficiaries, such as the charity or a spouse, for a specific period of time; at the end of that time period, the charity receives whatever is left in the trust.

Charitable Lead Trust — Also known as a front trust; gives the charity a specific gift before all other beneficiaries receive anything.

Clauses — The sections in your will that organize the information in a specific order.

Coach — These trained professionals specialize in offering financial, professional, and personal guidance to help you identify and manage monetary, career, and personal goals. There are certification courses for various forms of coaching, but there are no national standards, and formal training is not required to present oneself as a coach.

Codicil — A separate legal document that adds provisions to your existing will.

Cost-of-living Adjustment — Some plans have a variable that will allow for annual increases in the payments made to the employee to help cover the cost of rising prices. Not all plans have this feature.

Crummey Trust — An extremely complicated trust normally set up in conjunction with an irrevocable life insurance trust to make the payments for a life insurance policy; this is the kind of trust that requires an estate-planning attorney.

Custodian Account — This account for minor children, which can be in the form of a trust, allows you to deposit money or property in an account set up by a bank or brokerage firm. You can name yourself as the custodian, or trustee, of the account while you are alive and then name a successor to take over those responsibilities after you die.

- **Uniform Transfer for Minors Act (UTMA)** — This is the most current federal regulation that defines and allows an account, or trust, to be set up for minor children; if a state adopted this regulation, it served to repeal their UGMA statute. Michigan has adopted this regulation into law.
- **Uniform Gift to Minors Act (UGMA)** — This is the first federal regulation that defined and allows an account, or trust, to be set up for minor children; some states still have this form of the law on their books.

D

Decedent — A person who has died.

Disability Insurance — A disability insurance policy that will make payments to you to cover living expenses and replace your lost income as a result of your inability to hold a job.

- **Short-term Disability** — Provides benefits for about three months; some plans go a little longer, but only for a short period of time.
- **Long-term Disability** — Provides benefits for years but does eventually end, frequently at age 65, when you become eligible for social security.

Disclaimer — A refusal of a beneficiary to accept the gift given; recognized by both federal and state authorities if given in writing by a specific deadline, typically nine months after the donor's death.

Discretionary Trust — Gives a trustee the ability to distribute income and property to a variety of beneficiaries; he or she also has the option to control the distributions to a single beneficiary as he or she decides is appropriate.

Distribution — This is the disbursement or payment of property from an account to a beneficiary; it could be in the form of a check or some other monetary payment, or the transfer of a title into the name of the beneficiary.

Distribution Provisions — Any clause that identifies who will receive the income and the frequency of those distributions, such as payments made every April 15 to the IRS.

DNR — Do not resuscitate; an advanced medical directive that expresses your wish to not be resuscitated or revived if you appear to have died.

Donee — The person or institution receiving a gift.

Donor — The person who gives a gift or bequest.

Dumpster Diving — A slang term used to describe the act of digging through trash to find bills, bank statements, or other documents with account information or any personal information that might be useful to an identity thief; this is not considered an act of theft because the U.S. Supreme Court ruled that anything left out for trash collection is in the public domain.

Durable Power of Attorney — Allows an authorized person to act on behalf of the grantor of that power of attorney.

Dynasty Trust — Also known as a wealth trust; can last for several generations or be set up to never end. This kind of trust helps people with a vast amount of wealth control the distribution of that money and property over a long period of time.

E

Educational Trust — This is a kind of protective trust that sets aside money specifically for education-related expenses, such as tuition or training fees, books, or supplies. These trusts include provisions to stop payments if the student drops out of school or flunks numerous classes.

Ending Clauses — These include the legalities to meet statutory requirements so that your will is legal and valid, which include (but are not limited to) your signature, date, location of the signing, and witnesses.

Estate Planning — Creating a set of instructions about what should be done with your things — money, possessions, investments, collectibles, or anything you own — before and after you die.

Estate Tax — Referred to as the "death tax" by Congress, this is the federal tax on the property in your estate after you die.

Executor — Also called a personal representative, this is the individual who handles the property you are leaving behind. If you die without a will, the court appoints an administrator, frequently a spouse or child.

Exemption — This is a specific amount of money that will not be affected by estate taxes. Federal taxes and states with an estate tax often set an amount, such as $1 million, that is tax-free, then taxes are due on $1.01 million and beyond.

F

Family Consent — Also known as a health surrogate, this is a family member designated by state law who will make medical decisions for you when you cannot do it for yourself. These laws follow a specific order of kinship for who makes a decision. If you are married, your spouse, not your sister, will be your surrogate.

Family Trust — A legal arrangement that involves the transfer of property from the original owner to a family member for the purpose of holding and maintaining the property until the beneficiary takes ownership.

Fiduciary Powers Clause — A giving clause in your will that includes language giving your executor the power to serve as your executor, including any duties that go beyond the basic requirements in your state regulations.

Financial Planner — Certified Financial Planners (CFP), Chartered Financial Analysts (CFA), and some without initials are individuals who analyze the overall financial situation of an individual and then develop a comprehensive plan, in conjunction with the individual that will attempt to meet his or her financial goals and objectives. Planners who are certified have followed a specific course of education or training classes, and some go on to develop expertise in specific areas such as estate or retirement planning.

Funding a Trust — The placement of property in a trust; that same property will be called "trust principal" once it is under the auspices of the trust agreement.

G

Generation-Skipping Tax Transfer (GSTT) — This is a federal tax levied on property transferred to a person one or more generations removed from the donor.

Generation-Skipping Transfer Trust — A tax-saving trust that is designed to benefit multiple generations after you are gone.

Gift Tax — A federal tax levied against any property you give to another person or institution during a fiscal year; it can be in cash or the transfer of property, such as real estate or jewelry.

Giving Clauses — Explain what property goes to which person and under what circumstances. These can be as broad or explicit as you want. Real property clauses are statements that match up property with a person. Personal property clauses are used when you want to be explicit in your instructions. A residuary clause addresses the "leftovers" in your estate that you do not single out in a clause; this clause is essential for any kind of will to make sure that anything you forget or acquire since the will was prepared can be distributed. Making one or two beneficiaries is a good idea to keep your assets out of the hands of the courts.

Grantor-Retained Trusts — These are irrevocable, non-charitable trusts, which means they are set up in a way that is similar to a charitable trust, but the beneficiary is not a charity. There are three common types:

- **GRAT** — Grantor-retained annuity trust gives a fixed amount of money at predetermined times, often at regularly scheduled intervals.

- **GRIT** — Grantor-retained incomes trust designates specific people to receive certain property, such as stocks or a house, but the income or use of the property stays with you until your death.

- **GRUT** — Grantor-retained unit trust pays a specific percentage to the beneficiary.

Gross Estate — The value of all property owned by the deceased person on the date of that person's death; this is what gets taxed.

Guardian — The person legally appointed to be responsible for the needs of minor children until they reach a legal age; also, any adult who can be legally appointed to manage the affairs of an incompetent or infirm adult of any age.

Guardianship Clause — The appointment of a guardian for minor children (under the age of 18); a successor guardian should also be named as a backup.

H

Health Care Power of Attorney — Also known as medical power of attorney, this is the designation of a person who makes medical decisions for you when you cannot do it for yourself.

Heir — The legal title of a person who inherits property from an estate that does not have a will, or is intestate; beneficiaries are those who receive an inheritance by being named in a legal document, such as a will or trust.

Holographic Will — This is a handwritten document signed by you but not witnessed by anyone else. Some states, such as Michigan, recognize a handwritten will as valid; others do not, so you need to check your state laws if you want to use this kind of will.

Homeowner's Insurance — The exchange of premiums for a guaranteed payment to cover the loss of a house and other personal property in the residence. Other coverage can also be included, such as personal liability.

Homestead Exemption Statute — State law that protects a family home from being sold to pay off creditors if there is not enough money in an estate to cover outstanding debt.

I

Individual Retirement Arrangement (IRA) — An investment account that you set up for yourself for retirement savings. There is a limit to the contributions you can make annually. There is a tax deduction for making these contributions every year, so technically they are tax-free contributions.

- **Roth IRA** — Named after its primary legislative sponsor, Senator William Roth of Delaware. Contributions to this IRA are also tax-deductible in the year they are made, and taxes are paid when the money is withdrawn. The difference here is that the interest earned while the money is invested will be tax-free if you own the Roth IRA for at least five years.

Inheritance Tax — A state tax levied on the property received by a beneficiary.

Insurance — A method of protecting valuables in the form of a policy in which premiums are paid over time to guarantee a specific payment for a specific purpose by the company accepting the premiums. Those valuables can be property, such as your home, car, or jewelry; a person; the ability to work and care for yourself; life; health care; and long-term care.

Insurance Agent — An individual who is authorized by an insurance company to represent that company when dealing with an applicant for insurance, be it a medical, disability, dental, or long-term care policy. An agent can help you with your policy purchase by assessing the kind and amount of insurance you need and can afford.

Intestate — To die without a will.

Inter vivos Trust — A trust that is set up and takes effect during your lifetime, before your death.

Irrevocable — A trust that cannot be changed, no matter what.

J

Joint Will — This is one legal document for any two people, such as you and your spouse. The problem with this kind of will is that it is irrevocable, which means it cannot be changed after one of the two parties dies. The reason is that all decisions must be made by both people. A lawyer can tell you when this kind of will is a good idea, but most suggest separate wills to avoid complications.

Joint-with-survivor Pension — When an employee dies, his or her benefits will be paid to his or her spouse for the remainder of the spouse's life. If the spouse waives that right, then the employee's pension payments will be larger (no need to set aside extra money for future payments), and the pension payments end when the employee dies.

K

Keogh Plan — Pronounced "key-oh," this is a qualified retirement plan for sole proprietors and partners but can also be used by employees. The restrictions, distributions, and other details are similar to a defined contribution plan or defined benefit plan.

"Kiddie Tax" — The nickname used to describe an income tax applied to money that minors did not earn through employment, also called unearned income. The special laws passed in 1996 were created to close a loophole that allowed parents to give their children a large gift as a way to pay a lower tax on the interest earned; the child tax rate was significantly lower than the adult rate.

L

Lawyer — An individual who has completed a course of study in the law and passed a state certification exam that authorizes him or her to practice law and/or give legal advice. Also called attorneys, these individuals can specialize in specific aspects of estate planning, such as wills, trusts, or probate court, or they might have a more broad focus, such as estate planning or tax law.

Legal Title — Legal position that gives the trustee ownership of the property in a trust for the duration of the trustee's responsibility.

Liability — A debt or an obligation to pay money to another person or institution.

Life Insurance — A financial arrangement in which an individual makes payments on a policy that guarantees the payment of a specific amount of money to a beneficiary upon the death of the person who is covered by the policy.

Living Trust — Created while you are still alive, this trust allows you to be the grantor, trustee, and beneficiary if you choose; this is considered a will substitute as a way to avoid probate.

Living Will — Also known as a medical directive, this is a legal document in which you spell out the decisions you have made about your medical care while you are still alive.

Long-term Care Insurance — This insurance provides payments to cover the cost of medical care. In-home nursing or nursing home fees are examples of what might be covered.

M

Marital Dedication Trust — Puts property into a trust that is exclusively for your spouse, who decides what happens to the property after your death.

Medical Insurance — Frequently referred to as health insurance by those who sell it, the insurance that covers medical costs when you are sick and trying to cure an illness, injured, pregnant, and for regular checkups.

Medicaid — State-run medical insurance plan that is supported by federal funding and provides medical benefits that are minimal for the financially needy. To qualify for this plan, you have to possess no more than a set dollar amount in property.

Medicare — A medical insurance program offered by the federal government to people who are 65 or older, certain disabled people under the age of 65, and anyone with permanent kidney failure.

- **Part A** of this coverage is hospital insurance and **Part B** is medical insurance. Part B now comes with a monthly premium.

Medical Power of Attorney — Also known as health care power of attorney, this is the designation of a person who makes medical decisions for you when you cannot do it for yourself.

Minor Trust — A way to give gifts to a minor that avoids the gift tax and keeps the property safe until the minor becomes an adult and can take ownership of the trust.

Marital Trust — A trust for the surviving legal spouse of the deceased.

Mutual Will — A plan for your estate that is prepared in conjunction with another person.

N

Net Worth — A person's true financial value: Assets – Liabilities = Net Worth.

Non-Charitable Trust — A trust that has a person or institution that is not a charity as the beneficiary.

Non-Statutory Living Will — A legal document in which you spell out the decisions you have made about your medical care while you are still alive that does not comply with the laws of your state. A statutory document will likely provide more protection for the physicians and nurses carrying out your wishes.

Nuncupative Will — Also called an oral will, this is a spoken will. Some states only allow this kind of will if someone is literally on their deathbed, and it only covers personal property of little or no value. Again, you need to check with your state on the laws regarding this kind of will.

O

Opening Clauses — Lay out the basic information about who you are and set the stage for the clauses that follow. The introductory clause identifies you as the person who is making the will, the family statement clause introduces and identifies the family members who will be referred to later in the will, and the tax clause explains how the taxes on your estate will be paid.

Outright Charitable Gift — This is property you give to a charity and get nothing in return for; the gift can be cash or any other type of property.

Ownership — The individual(s) who hold the legal title to a piece of property; the ability to retain, sell, or give away this property depends on the number of people who hold that title, in some cases, their relationship, and any legal agreements/contracts connected to the property.

- **Sole Ownership** — A single person holds the title to the property.
- **Joint Ownership** — When any two people hold an equal share of the title to a piece of property; the most common form is spousal, or when a legally married couple has both names on a title to a piece of property.
- **Community Property** — A state law that views a wife and husband as equal partners and assumes a 50/50 split of ownership.
- **Separate Property** — Things owned by one spouse that are not part of the couple's community property.
- **Joint Tenancy** — A group of people who hold an equal and undivided title to a piece of property.

P

Payable-on-Death (POD) — An account, like a savings account, that has a specific stipulation that the death of the original owner automatically transfers the ownership to a named beneficiary.

Pension Benefit Guarantee Corporation (PBGC) — A federal agency that can insure and therefore protect some or all of your pension, if your plan qualifies for the coverage and your company purchases the insurance.

Pension Plan — A program that is set up by an employer, including government agencies, to pay employees benefits upon retirement. Each employee has an individual account, and the employer makes a contribution to each employee's account based on the terms of the plan. There are two common types of pension plans.

- **Defined Benefit Plan** — A plan in which the employee will receive a specified amount of money upon retirement; the amount of the disbursement made is based on the number of years of employment.
- **Defined Contribution Plan** — A pension plan that sets a specific amount an employee will put into the plan (a percentage of income) and makes payments only for the amount of money contributed to the plan.

Phishing — The act of fraudulently representing an e-mail, website pop-up window, or other electronic communication as being from a bank, some other financial institution, or a legitimate business that requests the verification of personal information. These communications also request "missing" information and updates to intentionally incorrect data.

Pour-over Will — This will place some property into a trust that was established while you were still alive.

Probate Court — The state-level court system that is specifically set up to handle all matters related to the distribution of a deceased person's estate; this is where a will is filed and unanswered questions about the disbursement of an estate are settled by a judge.

Profit-sharing Plan — Employees receive a portion of the profits earned by the company; the plan determines the amount that will be contributed to each employee's account.

Property — Also referred to as personal property, this comprises your possessions. This category is further divided into:

- **Real Property** — Any kind of real estate, such as a house, a condo, or a vacant lot.
- **Tangible Personal Property** — The things you can touch, such as a signed baseball, jewelry, or linen bed sheets.
- **Intangible Personal Property** — Checking accounts, savings accounts, money market funds, mutual funds, stocks, bonds, or retirement accounts such as a pension, an IRA, a Roth IRA, or a Keogh plan.

Property Guardian — Also known as a property manager, this is a legal adult who takes responsibility for the oversight of property inherited by a minor/child. Children under the age of 18 can inherit property, but they can only be allowed to legally own that property with adult supervision; an adult must have the responsibility of managing it.

Property Interest — This refers to the connection a person has to a specific item, piece of land, or other items.

- **Legal Interest** — This is property that a person can legally transfer or manage, but it is not owned by the individual. Someone who is responsible for the maintenance and oversight of the use of a piece of property but who does not legally own it is called a trustee.
- **Beneficial Interest** — You receive a benefit from the property.

Protective Trusts — These are designed with conditions to protect the beneficiary's property.

Provisions — Clauses that explain how you want your wishes carried out.

Q

QTIP — A qualified terminable interest property trust is a marital deduction trust, but instead of your spouse's deciding who gets the property after your death, the grantor makes that decision.

Qualified Pension Plan — A plan in which the amount of money that the employer puts into an employee's account is not taxed as income during the fiscal year the contribution is made.

R

Renter's Insurance — The exchange of premiums for a guaranteed payment to cover the loss of personal property housed in rental property that is used as a primary residence.

Revocable — A trust that can be changed.

S

Simple Will — A legal document that identifies whom you are, your beneficiaries, your executor, the directions you leave for the care of people for whom you are responsible, and the distribution of your assets.

Skimming — The act of using a special high-tech storage device to electronically "grab" account numbers and other information from a store computer register when a credit card transaction/purchase is processing.

Social Security Disability Benefit — Monthly payment made by the federal government to qualified recipients who can no longer work. Payments are made until the age of 65; at that point, you begin to receive the social security retirement benefit at the same rate.

Social Security Retirement Benefit — Monthly payment made by the federal government to qualified recipients who reach retirement age. Payments are based on contributions made during the individual's employment period.

Social Security Supplemental Security Income (SSI) — The federal government makes a monthly payment to qualified individuals. This benefit is for people who have little (if any) property or are blind or disabled in some other way.

Special Needs Trust — A support trust for a disabled person under the age of 65 (you or anyone else). This trust makes payments on the beneficiaries' behalf, as required by the state as reimbursement. After the beneficiary dies, the property in the trust is paid to other beneficiaries. This trust is designed to protect your property from seizure by the government or a creditor seeking reimbursement.

Special Provisions — Encompasses all clauses that create specific requirements that are unique to the beneficiary or the assets. For example, a beneficiary of a trust might be required to be 21 or graduate college before he or she can take ownership of that trust.

Spendthrift Trust — A trust that is set up for someone who will not be able to handle his or her own affairs or who is mentally incompetent, or might have financial problems and needs protection from creditors. The beneficiary does not own the property in the trust, just the payments that are made from the trust.

Spiritual Adviser — A minister, priest, monk, or some other cleric or individual trained in a specific faith tradition who offers guidance, support, and information related to their belief system.

Split-interest Trust — More than one individual benefits from the trust. One person or charity would have an interest in the trust for a specific period of time, and then another person or charity receives the property that remains.

State Estate Tax — A tax levied by the state on property left in an estate after a person dies, similar to the estate tax by the federal government, but the state tax is an additional tax burden. Not all states have an estate tax.

State Gift Tax — A tax by individual states according to terms the state sets that is levied against any property you give to another person or institution during a fiscal year; it can be in cash or the transfer of property, such as real estate or jewelry. Many of these are tied in some way to the federal estate tax.

State Income Tax — A tax on income earned during a fiscal year that is for residents of that state. Income earned in another state might be taxable in your state of residence, and any inheritance you receive that counts as income and is entered on your federal tax form can also be taxed.

Statutory Living Will — A legal document in which you spell out the decisions you have made about your medical care while you are still alive that complies with the statutes or laws of your state. A statutory document will likely provide more protection than a non-statutory living will for the physicians and nurses carrying out your wishes.

Stock Bailout — The transfer of stock ownership from your name to that of a charity; the fair market value of the stock at the time of the transfer is the gift amount.

Stock Bonus Plan — A retirement plan established by an employer to give shares of the company's stock to employees. When the employee receives the shares, he or she must pay taxes based on the value of the stock.

- **Employee Stock Ownership Plan (ESOP)** — A retirement type of stock bonus plan. The employer contributes shares of its stock to a qualified trust, and the employee only pays taxes based on distributions she receives.

Successor Trustee — Someone who will step in if the primary trustee is unable to serve or cannot continue to manage your trust. This person will have the same legal obligations for managing the trust as the original trustee, should the successor assume the management responsibilities.

Supplemental Needs Trust — A support trust for a handicapped, elderly, or disabled person in need of support is assisted by this trust in such a way that it does not reduce or jeopardize the eligibility of that person to receive public or private benefits. This trust is designed to protect your property from seizure by the government or a creditor seeking reimbursement.

Support Trust — Requires a trustee to pay only the income and property necessary to cover the cost of education or assistance such as health care fees or nursing home fees of the beneficiaries.

Survival Clause — This leaves everything in your estate to one named person. Married people frequently do this to ensure that everything goes to the surviving spouse.

Survivor Benefit — A portion of the deceased employee's pension paid to the surviving spouse. The amount, regularly a percentage, is set by the terms of the pension plan rules.

T

Tax-deferred — The taxes on money put into an investment account are paid when it is received by the employee in the form of a distribution, not at the time the money goes into the account.

Term Insurance — A life insurance policy that carries an annual premium and pays a specified death benefit to the beneficiary but does not have a cash value, so you cannot borrow money from it. The only payment made is to the beneficiary. The death benefit is not paid if premium payments are stopped.

- **Annual Renewable** — A term life policy that has an annual premium and can be renewed from year to year; be sure you understand the renewal rights before signing.
- **Decreasing** — A term life policy in which premiums remain the same, but the benefit decreases over time. For example, if you purchase this kind of insurance (also called mortgage or credit term insurance) to pay off your debts after you die, the mortgage you want to insure might be $250,000 at the time you purchase the insurance, but the mortgage value when you die might be $150,000. The policy then pays $150,000. This kind of insurance is recommended only for those who cannot get any other kind of insurance.
- **Level** — A term life policy with coverage that is guaranteed for a specific period of time, or term, such as five, ten, or 20 years at a specific premium. The premium will remain for the five-year period, but at year six, it will go up and remain at that rate through the tenth year, continuing after that.
- **Group** — Employers frequently purchase a term life policy for each employee as an added benefit. Employees get an excellent low rate, and there is no income tax on the premiums for the first $50,000 of coverage.

Testamentary Trust — A fund created by the terms of your will after your death.

Testamentary Trust Will — This will moves your assets into one or more trusts after your death.

Testator — A person who writes a will.

Totten Trust — This is a bank account that, upon your death, immediately passes to the named beneficiary.

Trust — A legal arrangement that involves the transfer of property from the original owner to a person or a company for the purpose of holding and maintaining the property for the benefit of a specific individual, group of people, or institution(s).

Trustee — The person or company that will oversee or manage a financial resources account, such as a trust or custodian account, once it is established. This person or group will make sure the property in the trust is safe and in good order until it is turned over to the beneficiary.

Trust Agreement — The legal document that spells out the terms of a trust, including the people and conditions and the rules that must be followed; some are state or federal laws, and others are specific conditions.

Trustor — The person who sets up the trust. Other names commonly used are creator, donor, settlor, or grantor.

Trust Principal — The name given to property that is placed into a trust and is managed by a trust agreement.

U

Umbrella Liability Insurance — The exchange of premiums for a guaranteed payment to cover a host of situations that would put personal property at risk, such as personal liability or negligence.

Uniform International Wills Act — Included in the Michigan Probate Code to cover wills prepared out of the country.

V

Vested — To meet the predetermined requirements contained within a pension plan based on the number of years you have worked for the employer. Before an employee can receive any distributions or take full ownership of a pension plan, the employee has to be fully vested.

W

Waiver — A written statement declining the right to receive benefits signed by a spouse. This waiver must be signed to legally sever the right to claim any benefits — an alternative agreement, such as signing a prenuptial agreement, will not be enough.

Whole Life Insurance — Sometimes called cash value life insurance, this is a form of life insurance for which the insured person pays a monthly or annual premium to a company that will, upon the owner's death, pay a predetermined, fixed amount of money to the beneficiaries. A portion of the fixed (meaning it will never go up or down) premium is invested, another portion is placed into an account, like a savings account, and that cash value is accessible to the policy owner. It can be borrowed against as a loan, or the cash can be taken as the proceeds of the policy instead of the death benefit payout.

- **Universal Life** — A kind of whole life policy that guarantees a minimum return, but the value of the policy can go up or down. If the policy makes more money, the return might be high enough to cover your premium payments.

- **Joint First-to-Die or Second-to-Die** — Just as it sounds, this is a policy held by two people, and the beneficiary is paid after the first or second person dies, as designated in the policy.

Will — A legal document in which you identify what people or institutions will receive money and property from your estate after your death; it also serves to appoint guardianship of children or adults who are your legal responsibility and designates an executor to manage your estate after you die.

Will Substitute — An agreement, contract, or other legal arrangement that will accomplish the same goals of a will — to protect and transfer property rights — but without the use of a will document.

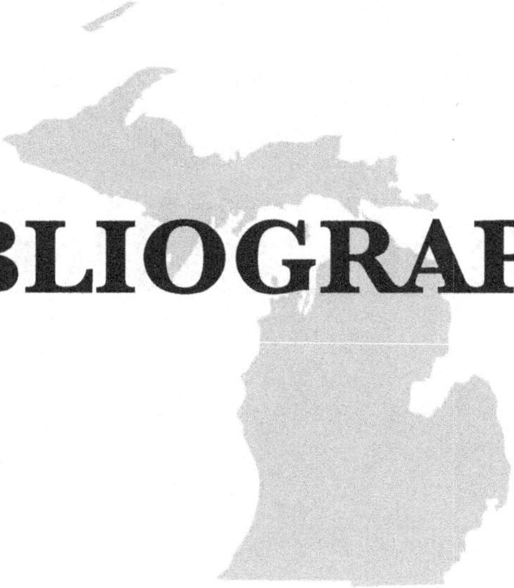

BIBLIOGRAPHY

Geller, Bradley. *Advance Directives: Planning for Medical Care in the Event of Loss of Decision-Making Ability.* State Bar of Michigan, **www.michbar.org/elderlaw/adpamphlet.cfm**. Accessed May 8, 2010.

Gift Tax. Internal Revenue Service. **www.irs.gov/businesses/small/article/0,,id=164872,00.html.** Accessed January 26, 2010.

Homestead Exemptions and Forms, What are homestead exemption laws?? **www.uslegalforms.com/realestate/homestead/.** Accessed May 7, 2010

Majority of American Adults Remain without Wills New Lawyers.com Survey Finds. Harris Interactive. **www.harrisinteractive.com/news/newsletters/clientnews/2007_Lawyers.pdf.** Accessed January 26, 2010.

Michigan Probate Code.

Michigan Taxes. Michigan Department of Treasury. **www.michigan.gov/taxes/0,1607,7-238-44143-156393--,00.html.** Accessed May 6, 2010.

U.S. Department of Labor. Bureau of Labor Statistics. **http://www.bls.gov.** Accessed January 26, 2010.

BIOGRAPHY

Linda C. Ashar is a lawyer, educator, horse breeder, freelance writer, and artist. Her law practice encompasses more than 29 years before the Ohio and Federal Bars. She is a senior shareholder in the firm of Wickens, Herzer, Panza, Cook, & Batista Co. in Avon, Ohio. In addition to her Juris Doctor in law, she has a Master of Arts in special education and a Bachelor of Arts in English. She is an adjunct professor at DeVry University and a frequent speaker at law seminars.

She is a professional writer and has authored *101 Ways to Score Higher on Your LSAT: What You Need to Know About the Law School Admission Test Explained Simply* (Atlantic Publishing Group, Inc. 2008), poetry, and several magazine and journal articles.

She and her lawyer-husband, Mike, operate Thornapple Farms in Vermilion, Ohio, where they breed Morgan Horses, including rare Lippitt Morgan bloodstock, Connemara Ponies, and Irish Kerry Bog Ponies, a critically endangered breed. Ashar serves on several nonprofit boards and is co-founder of Elysian Fields: The Justin Morgan Association for Retired Equines and the American Kerry Bog Pony Society.

Her interpretive art has been showcased by Mac Worthington Gallery in Columbus, Ohio; she paints, by private commission, subjects including equines, portraits, and landscapes. Reach her at ashar@hbr.net or lashar@wickenslaw.com.

Index

Made in the USA
Monee, IL
04 November 2026

67384910R00164